CATHOLICITY
AND
THE CHURCH

JOHN MEYENDORFF

CATHOLICITY
AND
THE CHURCH

ST. VLADIMIR'S SEMINARY PRESS
CRESTWOOD, NEW YORK 10707

By the same author

GREGORY PALAMAS: Defense of the Holy Hesychasts
    Text and French translation (1959; 2nd ed. 1974)
THE ORTHODOX CHURCH (1961; 2nd ed. 1981)
A STUDY OF GREGORY PALAMAS (1964)
ORTHODOXY AND CATHOLICITY (1966)
MARRIAGE: AN ORTHODOX PERSPECTIVE (1971; 2nd ed.
    1975)
BYZANTINE THEOLOGY (1974)
ST. GREGORY PALAMAS AND ORTHODOX SPIRITUALITY
    (1974)
BYZANTINE HESYCHASM: HISTORICAL, THEOLOGICAL
    AND SOCIAL PROBLEMS (1974)
CHRIST IN EASTERN CHRISTIAN THOUGHT (1975)
LIVING TRADITION (1978)
BYZANTIUM AND THE RISE OF RUSSIA (1980)
THE BYZANTINE LEGACY IN THE ORTHODOX CHURCH
    (1982)

Library of Congress Cataloging in Publication Data

Meyendorff, John, 1926-
   Catholicity and the church.

   Includes index.
   1. Orthodox Eastern Church—Doctrines—Addresses,
essays, lectures. 2. Theology—Addresses, essays,
lectures. I. Title.
BX320.2.M473   1983   230'.19   83-20218
ISBN 0-88141-006-3

CATHOLICITY AND THE CHURCH

© copyright 1983
by
ST. VLADIMIR'S SEMINARY PRESS

ISBN 0-88141-006-3

PRINTED IN THE UNITED STATES OF AMERICA

Contents

INTRODUCTION   7

CHAPTER I
THE THEOLOGY OF THE HOLY SPIRIT   15
  1. The Spirit in the Trinity   16
  2. The Spirit in man   21
  3. The Spirit in the Church   26

CHAPTER II
GREEK PHILOSOPHY AND CHRISTIAN
THEOLOGY IN THE EARLY CHURCH   31
  1. Origen and Augustine   34
  2. The Transfiguration of Hellenism   38
  3. Byzantium and Hellenism   42
  Conclusion: Catholicity and Tradition   46

CHAPTER III
CHURCH AND MINISTRY   49
  1. The Origins of the Episcopal Ministry   51
  2. Orthodox Attitudes in History   56
  3. The Ministry and the Church Today   59

CHAPTER IV
THE SIGNIFICANCE OF THE REFORMATION
IN THE HISTORY OF CHRISTENDOM   65

CHAPTER V
DOES CHRISTIAN TRADITION HAVE A FUTURE?   83
  Tradition and Eschatology   85

Tradition in the Second Century   89
The Contemporary Ecumenical Situation   93

CHAPTER VI

MISSION, UNITY, DIASPORA   103

CHAPTER VII

ONE BISHOP IN ONE CITY   111
    The Canons   111
    The Nature of the Church   116
    Conclusion   119

CHAPTER VIII

THE COUNCIL OF 381 AND
THE PRIMACY OF CONSTANTINOPLE   121
    1. Historical context   121
    2. Canonical meaning   127
    3. Ecclesiological significance   133
    4. Contemporary problems   138

CHAPTER IX

RUSSIAN BISHOPS AND CHURCH
REFORM IN 1905   143

INDEX   157

Introduction

The term "catholicity" is a neologism. In early Christianity, and until the modern period, Christian texts rather speak of the *Catholic Church* and so do not use the noun "catholicity" as an abstract concept. The first author to use the term "catholic Church" was St. Ignatius of Antioch (ca. 100 AD) who, in his letter to the Smyrnaeans wrote: "Where Jesus Christ is, there is the catholic Church" (*Smyrn.* 8:2).

What he meant to proclaim is the fullness and the universality of salvation revealed in Christ within the Church. The specific expression he discovered to define the Church became so popular that it was used in creeds—including the most definitive creedal formula approved by the ecumenical councils of Nicaea and Constantinople—in spite of the fact that the word "catholic" was not found in Scripture. Its meaning was derived from the Greek adverb καθ᾽ ὅλον (*kath'holon*), "in reference to the whole." According to St. Ignatius, the "catholic" Church was that Christian assembly which had accepted the whole of the divine presence in Christ, the whole truth, the fullness of life, and had assumed a mission directed at the salvation of the whole of God's creation. Although, in later times, the adjective "catholic" was used as synonymous with "universal," it is obvious that its original meaning did not refer to geography. "Catholicity" was a sign of the presence of *Christ,* and Christ, in His Word and in the mystery of the Eucharist, was present "wherever two or three" were gathered in His name (Mt. 18:20), in each local community of Christians.

However, the use of the adjective "catholic" clearly implied that some other gatherings of people who called themselves Christians lacked the "wholeness" of Christ. These were the "heretics" (splitters of the truth) or the "schismatics" (dividers of the community). So, gradually, the term "catholic" was used as an equivalent of "orthodox," which designated the holders of "right opinions," who rightly glorified God within the unity and holiness of the Spirit and in conformity with the original apostolic faith. The specificity of the original meaning was nevertheless realized by translators of the Creed. In most languages, the original, Greek term "catholic" was simply transliterated, not translated. The major exception is the Slavic version of the Creed of Nicaea-Constantinople, where the translators (St. Cyril and St. Methodius, or their immediate disciples) took the daring step of using the Slavic term *sobornaya tser'kov'* for "catholic Church." It is rather unlikely that they had in mind all the implications of the theology of *sobornost'*, conceived by nineteenth-century Russian theologians. Their use of the term may rather have been inspired by the liturgical vocabulary of their times, which designated the main assembly place of a local church or monastery as the *katholikon*, as distinct from smaller temples or *martyria*, where the eucharistic liturgy was celebrated only on days when a particular martyr or saint was commemorated. The *katholikon*, on the contrary, was the place of the regular Sunday Eucharist: it was the church of Christ and all His saints, living or dead, united in the eschatological event of the Lord's Day. In fact, the roots of the Slavic term *sobornaya tser'kov* lead back directly to the ecclesiology of St. Ignatius. Of course, this original meaning did not exclude the particular and rich intuitions of A. S. Khomyakov and his group in the nineteenth century about the Church as assembly or "council" (*sobor*), and about the "conciliar" nature of the Christian faith. Indeed, that faith, as Khomyakov saw, is not the knowledge of an individual, but a vision implying *communion* in the Spirit with the saints of all ages and all places. This is an essential dimension of catholicity.

This history of the term "catholic" and its various implications has been studied and discussed by many authors.[1] Our

[1]A special Orthodox theological conference on the subject was held in

intention in this book was not to start this discussion again, but to gather together papers and articles delivered or published on various occasions and concerned in every case with expressions of catholicity in the Orthodox Church today, both in its inner life and in its relationships with other Christians and the world at large.

Indeed, the use of the noun "catholicity," as a somewhat abstract category, replacing the concrete reality signified by St. Ignatius of Antioch when he wrote of the "catholic Church," is itself symptomatic of a gradual evolution of ecclesiology. In the minds of Orthodox Christians, the "church" came to signify simply the local parish ("our church"); or, in America, a particular ecclesiastical jurisdiction; or a national church ("the Greek church," "the Serbian church"); or a denomination, so that the term "catholic" is associated with Roman Catholicism, and some Orthodox go as far as defensively objecting to its application to Orthodoxy. All this denotes not only a large degree of ignorance but also a spiritual loss and a danger for the true faith. The concrete and direct implications of our confessing a belief in the "one, holy, catholic, and apostolic Church" are lost, and are replaced by a vague and imaginary, or a narrowly confessional, concept of "catholicity," coupled with, in practical terms, a congregational, Protestant, or sectarian understanding of church life.

The title of the present collection of nine essays—*Catholicity and the Church*—by placing these two words side by side, attempts to focus attention on the problems created by their opposition to each other. All the essays contain an implicit affirmation addressed first to the Orthodox themselves, but also to those involved in ecumenical groups. There is no way in which one can claim to be a Christian except through concrete membership in the Catholic Church and through a continuous effort at manifesting the catholicity of the Church.

Orthodox Christians often take Orthodoxy for granted by identifying it simply with a formal preservation of the right

Crestwood, NY, at St. Vladimir's Seminary, under the auspices of the Orthodox Theological Society of America, September 25-30, 1972. The papers were published in *St. Vladimir's Theological Quarterly* 17 (1973): 1-2.

doctrinal statements, or, worse, by reducing it to ethnic affiliation, or to some other limited, human criterion. Such reductions of Orthodox churchmanship make it impossible to present to non-Orthodox Christians or to secular society a plausible claim to catholicity.

What we have to recover is the sense, implied already very clearly by St. Ignatius in his famous sentence quoted above, that it is *Christ,* through the Spirit, who makes the Church to be "catholic," whereas no human group, however worthy, holy, and active, is able to "create" catholicity: it can only cooperate (cf. the patristic *synergeia*) with divine grace and manifest (or fail to manifest) the divine concern for the life and salvation of the world. Obviously, at no time in history, not even in apostolic times, could the human communities of believers which constituted the "catholic" churches everywhere be fully adequate to the task. It is this sense of historical inadequacy which makes most Protestants today believe that, concretely and empirically, no single church or denomination —not even all Christians together—can legitimately claim *to be* the Catholic Church: they can only be its partial manifestations. Thus, in the widely-accepted Protestant understanding, "ecumenical" involvement implies the abandonment of doctrinal exclusivity, the practice of "intercommunion," and the realization that "catholicity" is actually shared (perhaps in different degrees) by all the divided Christian denominations.

For the Orthodox, the problem is different. The four marks of the Church—oneness, holiness, catholicity, and apostolicity—are understood as coming from Christ and the Holy Spirit. Consequently, the Church herself cannot be "more or less" one or "more or less" catholic. She is what Christ and the Spirit make her to be. In her being she is not man-made. Human beings and human communities can rebel against her, but they cannot change her being.

Such rebellions are of two different orders. On the one hand, entire local churches can commit themselves, permanently and officially, to a wrong doctrine, or can substantially modify their sacramental and apostolic structure: in this case, there is heresy or schism, the very opposite of catholicity. But, on the other hand, there can also be passive neglect, unconscious betrayal, and, through weakness, surrender before "powers and principalities." The Orthodox Church can indeed claim to be "orthodox" and "catholic" only in as much as she has never, formally and authoritatively, replaced apostolic truth with false doctrine or officially endorsed substitute norms of catholicity. Such false doctrines or substitutions are what Orthodoxy reproaches non-Orthodox Christians for. However, this purity in formal commitment does not mean that Orthodox Christians are not guilty of countless betrayals of the second order. Enjoying the humanly undeserved privilege of belonging to the Church which never formally strayed from catholic tradition, we, the Orthodox Christians of the twentieth century, present to the world an image of divisiveness, of theological unawareness, of missionary passivity, of dependence upon socio-political concerns.

The catholicity of the Church—so obviously manifested in the Orthodox liturgy, in the Orthodox canonical tradition, in Orthodox theology—is nevertheless hidden by systematically inconsistent attitudes adopted in practice. Never before in the history of Christianity has the Orthodox tradition, present today on all the continents, had a better opportunity to witness, to promote the Christian message, to be understood and experienced by entire peoples and civilizations which had never before been in contact with it. The contemporary ecumenical movement in particular is a major opportunity and an unprecedented forum where the Orthodox can not only witness to their faith, but also, simply by loving those who share the name of Christian, learn how to express more fully and more completely the catholicity of their Church. Actually, the rather critical state of ecumenism today—especially in its organized and bureaucratic forms—is, at least partially, due to the inability of the Orthodox to express their message in an effective way, with sufficient love to make the hard truth accepted and understood by those who miss it.

Such are the feelings which justify—in the eyes of this author—the publication of the following nine studies in a single book. Each of them was originally delivered as a paper and was followed by discussion, in which religiously mixed audiences participated. The final versions published here reflect the thought of the author as it developed in the framework of such living encounters. They are not academic exercises in abstract theologizing.

The first two chapters examine the ways in which the living Christian revelation meets the reality of a world created by God, but fallen and requiring a new birth in order to regain its original communion with the Creator: a new birth in the Spirit, the bestower of divine life, leading the human mind to be transformed and thus able to understand and express the trinitarian mystery. Without such transformation, no meaningful theology can exist today.

Chapters 3, 4, and 5 are dialogues with Christians of the Western traditions. They are based on the conviction that a) the tradition of the Christian West is not foreign to Orthodoxy simply because it is "Western," but because the schism with the East has created an unbalanced situation in which a lack of truly catholic conciliarity has lead to a one-sided overgrowth of peculiarly Western doctrines and institutions; b) the Protestant Reformation was a "protest" not against Orthodoxy but against a Roman and Latin Christendom which itself had gone out-of-balance after the schism with the East; c) the Orthodox witness, if it is truly orthodox and catholic, should be able to manifest that balanced *sensus ecclesiae* ("sense of the Church") which is the key to Christian unity.

The last four chapters are devoted to problems in the Orthodox Church herself, and particularly the disastrous spectacle of Orthodox divisiveness in areas falsely designated as the "diaspora." Indeed, this divisiveness contradicts the very clear requirements of Orthodox ecclesiology and canon law. It witnesses to a conscious unwillingness by Orthodox leadership to lead its flock in accordance with Church Tradition, with the result that the Orthodox Church seems, in the eyes of the contemporary world, to refuse her mission of being *the Church* for all mankind. One of the canonical tools which could be very useful under the circumstances is provided by "ancient custom" (τὰ ἀρχαῖα ἔθη, Council of Nicaea, canon 6) in the traditional primacy of the ecumenical patriarchate of Constantinople. Chapter 8 discusses the origin of that primacy and the realistic ways in which it could be exercised today.

The final chapter is a case study of the remarkable attempt at self-reformation made early in this century by the largest of the autocephalous Orthodox Churches, the Church of Russia. It should now be read together with the more recent publications on the subject, especially those by James Cunningham (*A Vanquished Hope: The Movement for Church Renewal in Russia, 1905-1906*, Crestwood, NY: St. Vladimir's Seminary Press, 1981) and by Dimitry Pospielovsky (*The Russian Church under the Soviet Regime, 1917-1982*, 2 vol., Crestwood, NY: St. Vladimir's Seminary Press, 1983). Modern readers will discover the extraordinary vitality of Russian Orthodoxy in pre-revolutionary years, and particularly its readiness for self-criticism and self-reform. By learning more about the facts which preceded the bloodbath of martyrdom in the twenties and thirties, many Westerners may modify their somewhat limited vision of Orthodoxy as a spiritually frozen tool of caesaropapism.

John Meyendorff

CHAPTER I

The Theology of the Holy Spirit*

Of all the aspects of Christian thought, the theology of the Holy Spirit is the one which fits with the greatest difficulty into a preconceived systematic scheme. Its mysterious implications are well expressed in the unusual character of the Byzantine liturgical hymnography for Pentecost—both affirmative and dynamic:

The Holy Spirit was, is, and ever shall be
Without beginning, without end,
Forever united and numbered with the Father and
the Son.
Life and life-creating, Light and Giver of Light,
Good in Himself, the Fountain of Goodness,
Through whom the Father is known and the Son is
glorified . . .
One power, one order, one worship of the Holy
Trinity. . . .

The Spirit is the deifying God;
Fire proceeding from Fire,
Speaking, acting, distributing gifts.
By the Spirit the prophets, apostles and martyrs
are crowned.
Strange is this report! Strange is this sight!   (Vespers)

*Talk delivered at General Theological Seminary, New York, under the auspices of the Trinity Institute, on March 21, 1982.

This hymnography, which still reflects the spontaneous character of the homilies of St. Gregory of Nazianzus of which it is a paraphrase, conveys the charismatic nature of the Christian experience, but it also points at its trinitarian and ecclesial dimensions. The Spirit is not only inspiring prophecy, He also is the source of "power" and of "order." Furthermore, He is coeternal with the Father and the Son, and thus a personal and divine source of "deification" (θέωσις).

These various aspects obviously cannot be integrated into a philosophically and intellectually rational *system*: they rather are "a strange sight," as the liturgical poet exclaims.

However, the unsystematical character of the patristic and Eastern Christian thought about the Holy Spirit does not imply an absence of some basic, fundamental affirmations. Without these the experience of the Spirit would lack authenticity. Within the limits of this paper, I am, of course, obliged to be quite selective, and to restrict myself to simply pointing at three dimensions: the trinitarian nature of God, the "spiritual" element in man, and the role of the Spirit in the Church and in the world.

1. *The Spirit in the Trinity*

The affirmation that the Spirit is not only a "gift" of divine grace, but is also—together with the Father and Son —the divine and personal *Giver* of life and sanctification, was made with particular force toward the end of the Arian disputes of the fourth century in the *Letters to Serapion* of St. Athanasius and the remarkable book *On the Holy Spirit* by St. Basil. It has been often noted that trinitarian personalism was essential in the theology of the Cappadocian fathers and in the Orthodox tradition of later centuries. As G. L. Prestige noted: "The groundwork of their thought lay in the triplicity of equal hypostases, and the identity of the divine *ousia* came second in order of prominence to their minds."[1]

This priority of trinitarianism over the notion of divine unity was not, however, a matter of philosophical persuasion.

[1]*God in Patristic Thought* (London: SPCK, 1952) pp. 242-3.

It was not an intellectual attitude only. Rather, it was based on a reading of the New Testament, which implied that the first characteristic and content of the Christian kerygma was an encounter with God as three persons. The Arian controversy was essentially about the identity of Jesus Christ: the Nicaean faith affirmed His divine identity and His "consubstantiality" with the Father, because only God can truly be *Savior*. All the authority and effectiveness of His words and actions depended upon this identification: only God can communicate divine life to created human beings. The true foundation stone of the Christian faith is therefore Peter's answer to Christ's question, "Who do you say that I am?": "The Son of the living God" (Mt 16:15-16).

In the theology of Athanasius and Basil, the identity of the Holy Spirit is demonstrated by the same logic. Since the Spirit is inseparable from the Son in the baptismal formula; since His action reveals Jesus as Christ, and renders His presence effective in the world; since, together with the Father and the Son, He is the source of one of the three gifts listed in 2 Cor 13:14 ("the grace of the Lord Jesus Christ and the love of God the Father and the fellowship of the Holy Spirit"), the Spirit is indeed a person, or hypostasis, of the divine Trinity. He spoke personally to Philip (Acts 8:29), to Peter (Acts 10:19; 11:12), to the church of Antioch (Acts 13:2), and to apostolic council of Jerusalem ("It has seemed good to the Holy Spirit and to us" Acts 15:28).

The Creed of Nicaea-Constantinople reflects very clearly this trinitarian personalism, which the party of the so-called "Neo-Nicaeans," headed by the Cappadocian Fathers, promoted so successfully. The Spirit "is worshipped and glorified together with the Father and the Son." However, the text of the Creed somehow avoids applying the word "God" to the Spirit. Indeed, the Spirit is worshipped "together with" God the Father Almighty, and "together with" the Son who is "true God of true God," but He is called only "the Lord, the Giver of Life." One can remember, of course, that the same reserve (the same *oikonomia*) is apparent in Basil's book on the Spirit. Basil avoided the use of the word "God" in reference to the Holy Spirit, and was even chided by his friend, St. Gregory of Nazianzus, for this omission (see below, chapter 8). Whatever the historical reasons for it, the drafters of the Creed also considered the divinity of the Spirit is affirmed with sufficient clarity by a simple quotation from Jn 15:26: "Who proceeds from the Father."

Indeed, in the Cappadocian conception of the Trinity, the Father is seen as the personal (or "hypostatic") origin of divine existence. In the Middle Ages this was the major theological objection of the Orthodox East to the Western interpolation of the Creed by the words "and from the Son" (*filioque*). More particularly, the Greeks rejected the arguments which were proposed by Latin theologians to justify the doctrine of the "double procession" of the Spirit "from the Father and the Son" and which invoked the doctrine of consubstantiality. Such Latin arguments made it appear that the existence of the Spirit is not, primarily, a hypostatic, personal reality, proceeding from the person of the Father, but a manifestation of the common essence of the Father and the Son. Already Patriarch Photius, in the ninth century, objected to the "double procession," calling it modalistic, or "semi-Sabellian."[2]

It is not my purpose to describe here again the *filioque* controversy. Interestingly enough however, the issue has recently been debated once more within the Faith and Order Commission of the World Council of Churches and has provided the members with an opportunity to recognize the importance of trinitarianism for any aspect of the Christian faith.[3]

Almost inevitably, the debate between East and West on this subject always returns to the issue whether God is primarily to be conceived in His essential unity, or whether Christian experience and Christian theology should always begin with the personal existence of the Three. Indeed, the Cappadocian Fathers do not hesitate to describe the Trinity by the analogy of three human persons: "Peter, James, and

---

[2]*Mystagogy of the Holy Spirit* 9, 23; PG 102, cols. 289B, 313BC.
[3]Cf. L. Vischer, ed., *Spirit of God, Spirit of Christ: Ecumenical Reflections on the Filioque Controversy* (London: SPCK; Geneva: WCC, 1980).

John,"[4] or "Adam, Eve, and Seth."[5] Understandably, they faced the objection of their critics that they were actually preaching "tritheism." In the West, on the contrary, the central anthropomorphic analogy proposed by St. Augustine is his famous psychological image: "memory, intellect, will,"[6] three attributes of a single person. Here is the foundation for the Photian accusation of modalism.

Of course, it would be unfair to pass an ultimate judgment upon the two trinitarian models on the basis of such analogies, but the root of the problem is clearly visible, and it has a direct impact upon the theology of the Holy Spirit. However, another anthropological model was also used, which shows a measure of convergence between Augustine and the Eastern patristic tradition: it is the model of "the lover, the beloved, and love," which we find in St. Augustine,[7] but also in the great Byzantine theologian, St. Gregory Palamas. Palamas writes: "The Spirit of the Word is like a mysterious love of the Father towards the Word mysteriously begotten; it is the same love as that possessed by the Word . . . towards Him who begets Him; this He does in so far as He comes from the Father conjointly with [the Spirit as] love, and this love rests naturally on Him."[8]

The doctrine of the Trinity is the only real basis for the definition—found in 1 Jn 4:8—that "God is love." However, the divine love which unites the three divine Persons is also communicated to human persons, and this communication—or rather "communion" (κοινωνία), or even *theosis* —is the personal gift of the Spirit, as the gift of adoption to the Father in Christ.

In the Trinity itself, the Spirit proceeds from the Father and "rests" on the Son. The divine being is the Trinity: the Spirit does not proceed further, to a quaternity, or to a pantheistic merger of all beings within God. This "resting" upon the Son signifies that when the gifts of the Spirit are bestowed

---

[4]Gregory of Nyssa, *That there are not three gods*, ed. F. Mueller, in W. Jaeger, *Gregorii Nysseri Opera*, III, Leiden, 1958, p. 38.
[5]Gregory of Nazianzus, *Or.* 31, 11; PG 26, col. 145A.
[6]*De trinitate* 4, 30.
[7]Augustine, *De trinitate* 8, 14.
[8]*Physical Chapters* 36; PG 151, col. 1144D-1145A.

upon man, this always happens "in Christ"; they do not go
further than Christ, and are accessible only in Him. There is
no way of separating or isolating the Spirit from the Son,
from the "fullness of Divinity" which has been revealed in
Christ once and for all. It is such attempted separations which
lead to various reductions of the Christian message: the
notion of a "third covenant" of the Spirit, still forthcoming;
charismaticism, which opposes itself to a christocentric and
eucharistic understanding of the Church; the reduction of the
Christian experience to emotionalism, opposed to institution
and dogma, etc.

In the Holy Trinity, the Spirit unites and connects the
Father and the Son. And He also connects us with divine life.
But this connection is not the expression of an essentialist
view of God. It is not simply a manifestation of their "consubstantiality": it is a personal function, which also keeps
the Father and the Son as distinct persons, just as it preserves
the fully distinct personal existence of the human person
entering into communion with divine life.[9]

The divine personal identity of the "other Comforter"
sent by Christ from the Father is, therefore, the very basis
of the Christian doctrine of salvation, if one understands
salvation as the Greek fathers did in terms of communion
with divine life. This is well expressed in the liturgical tradition: the invocation of the Spirit at each sacramental action
and indeed at each action of worship; the trinitarian baptismal formula; the trinitarian structure of the eucharistic canons.
These dimensions of the theology of the Spirit become even
more evident when one considers the "theocentric" anthropology—determined by the doctrine of the image of God in
man—which was adopted and developed in the Greek patristic
tradition.

---

[9]This point is very well developed in Dumitru Staniloae, *Theology and the
Church*, chapter on "The Holy Trinity: Structure of Supreme Love", (Crestwood, NY: St. Vladimir's Seminary Press, 1980) pp. 96-97.

2. *The Spirit in man*

While maintaining the doctrine of the absolute trans-
cendence of God as Creator vis-à-vis all created nature, the
Greek Fathers also understood the ultimate destiny of man in
terms of *communion* with God, or "deification" (θέωσις).
Of course, the basic theological foundation for deification
is to be seen in the doctrine of the "hyposatic union" of divinity and humanity in Christ. Already Irenaeus wrote: "The
Word became what we are so that we might become what
He is,"[10] and the same striking affirmation is picked up by
Athanasius: "He was made man, so that we might be made
God."[11] However, this christological dimension is never
separable from pneumatology. The Incarnation is realized
through the Holy Spirit "overshadowing" Mary, the New
Eve, and its result, according to Irenaeus, is that the Word
"unites man to the Spirit . . . Placing the Spirit in man, He
Himself is made the head of the Spirit, and gives the Spirit
to be head of man."[12]

This concept of salvation is itself based upon an understanding of the human being which views the *natural* state
of man as composed of three elements: body, soul, and Holy
Spirit. Using a terminology very close to that of St. Paul,
Irenaeus sees the human reality as "composed of a body taken
from earth, and a soul which receives the Spirit from God."[13]
The Spirit is not seen here as a "supernatural" grace—added
to an otherwise "natural," created humanity—but as a function of humanity itself in its dynamic relationship to God, to
itself, and to the world. When the weakness of the flesh is
absorbed by the power of the Spirit, Irenaeus writes, then
man ceases to be carnal and becomes spiritual, because of his
communion with the Spirit.[14]

[10]*Against Heresies* 5, *praef.*; ed. Rousseau-Doutreleau' *Sources chrétiennes*
153 (Paris: Cerf, 1969), p. 14.
[11]*On the Incarnation* 54; PG 25, col. 192B.
[12]*Against Heresies* 5, 20, 2; ed. cit., p. 260.
[13]*Against Heresies* 3, 22, 1; ed. Rousseau-Doutreleau' *Sources chrétiennes*
211 (Paris: Cerf, 1974), p. 432.
[14]Ibid. 5, 9, 2; ed. cit., p. 110.

Obviously, Irenaeus is not concerned here with the opposition between "nature" and "grace," or even with distinguish-
ing the "Holy Spirit" from the created, human spirit. Actually,
the legitimacy of such distinctions was never fully accepted
even by the later Greek patristic writers. Gregory of Nazianzus speaks of an "efflux" of the Holy Spirit in man,[15] and
Gregory of Nyssa insists that what distinguishes the *human*
nature from the rest of Creation is precisely its *natural* congeniality with God.[16] "When God created Adam," writes
ps.-Macarius, "He did not give him bodily wings like the
birds, but prepared for him in advance the wings of the Holy
Spirit . . . to lift him up and carry him wherever the Spirit
wishes."[17]

Similar references could easily be multiplied, but the
question is that of the basic context in which they are to be
understood. It would probably be inaccurate to interpret them
against an exclusively neoplatonic background, implying a
dualism between spirit and matter. Quite to the contrary, it
is because the Fathers want to avoid that dualism that they
identify the human spirit with the divine *Holy Spirit,* Creator
of both soul and body. The references to the presence of the
Spirit in the *natural* man rather point to two things:

—the *openness upwards* of the human person, called to
ascend towards the divine, unending, limitless aim which
God has set as human destiny;

—the *freedom,* which Gregory of Nyssa identifies as the
very content of the image of God, making man similar to his
Creator and different from all other created beings.

The restoration of the Spirit as guiding principle of human
existence in Christ is therefore a return to "the ancient
dignity of freedom,"[18] which Adam lost through the Fall, by
becoming a slave to death, to corruptibility, and to sinfulness.
The Spirit restores what Maximus the Confessor called
"natural will" which gives man freedom from all cosmic

---

[15]*Poems*, PG 37, col. 452.
[16]*Catechetical Oration* 5; ed. J. H. Strawley (Cambridge, 1956), p. 23.
[17]*Homily* 5, 11.
[18]Gregory Palamas, *Triads for the defense of the holy hesychasts* 1, 1, 9;
ed. Meyendorff, 2nd ed. (Louvain, 1973) p. 27.

determinisms, and allows him to be truly himself in relation to God and the world.[19] The human person is authentically *free* only in unity with the Spirit of God.

It is at this point that one discovers why, beginning with the author of the writings attributed to St. Macarius the Great, the entire tradition of Eastern Christian spirituality insisted upon the *personal* and *conscious* character of the Christian experience of God. Addressing Constantinopolitan monks, the eleventh century mystic, St. Symeon the New Theologian, writes: "I entreat you, let us endeavour to see and contemplate Christ even in this life. For if we are found worthy to see Him here, we shall not die; death will have no dominion over us [Rom 6:9]. Let us not wait to see Him in the future, but strive to contemplate Him now."[20] For Symeon, the restoration of the human person by the Spirit is a restoration in full freedom, and that freedom refers not only to conversion as such, but to the entire Christian life which follows baptism and which is a constant ascent "from glory to glory." And this ascent is *natural* to man. He was created for it, and it alone can allow him also to accomplish his mission of subduing the earth (Gen 1:28) without being dominated by the cosmic powers.

Without the Spirit the human being is incomplete and imprisoned. This is why the liturgical language associated with the Spirit so often uses the image of human *thirst* being finally quenched.[21] This reflects baptismal symbolism, but also undoubtedly the experience of the natural inadequacy of Spirit-less, fallen humanity: there is no authentic human life without the Spirit, as there is no physical life without water.

This insistence on the role of the Holy Spirit in liberating the human person does not lead—if properly understood—to any form of spiritual individualism. Indeed, the theology of the Spirit is inseparable from the trinitarian context: the Spirit

[19]Cf. J. Meyendorff, *Christ in Eastern Christian Thought*, 2nd ed. (Crestwood, NY: St. Vladimir's Seminary Press, 1975) pp. 147-51.

[20]*Catechetical discourses* 2; ed. B. Krivocheine, *Sources chrétiennes*, 96 (Paris: Cerf, 1963) pp. 421-24; English trans. C. J. de Catanzaro (New York: Paulist Press, 1980) p. 58.

[21]Cf. P. Evdokimov, *L'Esprit saint dans la tradition orthodoxe* (Paris: Cerf, 1969) pp. 87-88.

reveals Christ and grants adoption to the Father. The coming of the "other Comforter" is an eschatological event manifesting and anticipating the *parousia* of Christ. The action of the Spirit is, in fact, an introduction to the life of the Trinity, which is love, reciprocity, communion, a union which does not suppress personal diversity. There is, between human persons, a legitimate, God-created and mutually enriching diversity which has its roots in the Trinity Itself.

One form of diversity recognized in the patristic tradition and particularly relevent to the theology of the Spirit is the distinction between man and woman. Does this distinction have any root in the very image of God in man? The answer to this question must of course exclude any idea of sexuality in the divine being, but this does not imply that, by creating man as male and female, God did not put His own stamp on that essential and basic duality in human nature. While it is always dangerous to use the doctrine of the image of God in man in terms of an anthropomorphism of God, the reverse is legitimate: man does reflect the being of God and his nature cannot be fully understood without reference to the divine model. Thus, in an anthropological context, it is possible to recall a long-standing tradition, which seems to go back primarily to early Syrian Christianity and which sees human feminity as rooted in a particular way in the person of the Holy Spirit. The idea may have come about naturally since the word for "spirit" is feminine in Syriac and in other Semitic languages. In any case, the great fourth-century spiritual author, Aphraates, speaks of man's love "for God, as Father, and the Spirit, as Mother."[22] The idea is also present in the *Hymns* of St. Ephrem the Syrian and the writings of some Greek spiritual authors. Thus, one reads in St. Anastasius of Sinai (seventh century): "Adam is the type and image [τύπος καὶ εἰκὼν] of the unoriginate almighty God, cause of all; the son born of him [Abel] manifests the image of the begotten Son and Word of God; and Eve, who proceeded from Adam, signifies the proceeding hypostasis of the Holy Spirit. This is why God did not breathe in her

[22]*Demonstration* 18, 11.

breath of life: she was already the type of the breathing and life of the Holy Spirit."[23]

Obviously, if such analogies are to serve the theological understanding of human existence, they are to be used only as analogies, just as the image which identifies the Spirit as "love" connecting the Father and the Son. However, the image of God in man is not a reality which applies only to the individual human being, but it must also involve the mutual relationships between human persons. It is therefore theologically legitimate to look for a divine model which would somewhat explain and justify the most fundamental and creative polarity of human nature. Within the framework of the patristic tradition, which is normative for an Orthodox theologian, the model must be sought in the trinitarian relations within God, and particularly in the theology of the Holy Spirit. Indeed, "the distinction between person and nature reproduces in humanity the order of divine life, expressed by the dogma of the Trinity."[24] There is no masculinity and feminity in God, but men and women carry the image of God not only in their identity, but also in their distinctiveness.

In His activity in creation and in salvation, the role of the Spirit is never inferior but always complementary to that of the Son, both preceding Him and completing or "sealing" the Son's acts. The Spirit never calls to Himself but to the Son, the God-man, the New Adam, the only One in whom the "hypostatic union" of divinity and humanity took place. The role of the Spirit in salvation (as also in the internal life of the Trinity) is "kenotic": it is always directed to the Other. The "Spirit of God was moving over the face of the waters" (Gen 1:2) at the very inception of creation. The Word, however, was the One "*by whom* all things were made," as the Creed states. The Word—not the Spirit—became flesh, yet it happened because the Holy Spirit came upon Mary (Lk 1:35). And it is again the Spirit who, within the Church, makes Christ eschatologically present in the midst of His disciples. Every baptism is "sealed" by the Spirit, who is also

[23]*On the image and likeness;* PG 89, col. 1145BC.
[24]V. Lossky, *Orthodox Theology: An Introduction* (Crestwood, NY: St. Vladimir's Seminary Press, 1978) p. 128.

invoked at every celebration of the Eucharist "to make" the bread and wine the Body and Blood of Christ. The saints also, while practicing the uninterrupted "Jesus prayer," define this activity as "the acquisition of the Holy Spirit" (St. Seraphim of Sarov, d. 1833).

3. The Spirit in the Church

It is again the essential thrust of early Christian thought, particularly as expressed by Irenaeus, which provides the basic key for a balanced understanding of the Spirit's action in the Christian community. As we have seen earlier, Irenaeus understands salvation as "new creation," through a new "insufflation" of the Spirit into man: "[A]t the beginning of our creation in Adam, the breath of life from God, united with created substance, animated man and made him a rational animal, so at the end the Word of the Father and the Spirit of God, united with the ancient substance of the creation of Adam, made a living and perfect man, receiving the perfect Father, so that as in the animal we were all dead, in the spiritual we are all made alive."[25] However, this new "insufflation" of the Spirit does not occur in the human individual, but happens within the total "recapitulation" of humanity, of which *the eucharistic assembly of the local church* is the concrete realization.

It is not possible for me to discuss here in detail the structure of the early Church as described by Irenaeus. But I would like to point out one shortcoming which appears in most commentaries on his famous doctrine of apostolic tradition, because this shortcoming is precisely connected with the doctrine of the Spirit. In such commentaries, the doctrine of tradition is envisaged retrospectively: it affirms a continuity with the past, i.e. with the witness of the apostles of Jesus, as transmitted and taught by a succession of bishops. Indeed, in Irenaeus this notion of a *public* and ecclesiastical tradition is one of his most potent arguments against the gnostic

[25]*Against Heresies* 5, 1, 3; ed. cit. p. 26; trans. Cyril C. Richardson, *Early Christian Writers* (New York: Macmillan, 1970) p. 387.

notion of *secret* traditions, transmitted from one charismatic individual to another. However, this retrospective continuity of tradition—a sort of anamnesis of the redemptive acts of Christ—is inseparable, in Irenaeus, from the activity of the Spirit which is invoked (*epiclesis*) by the Church, and which alone transforms the reality of the past into a *presence of the eschaton.* Such is, indeed, the essential meaning of the eucharistic celebration, as expressed with brilliant clarity by John Zizioulas: ". . . the Spirit is the one who brings the eschata into history. He confronts the proceeds of history with its consummation, with its transformation and transfiguration. . . . [T]he Church's *anamnesis* acquires the eucharistic paradox . . . the *memory of the future.*"[26]

If this is so, the structure of the Church itself, its ministries and their functions, must be determined not only by a concern for retrospective continuity with apostolic times, but also by the eschatological nature of the recapitulation of humanity, accomplished by Christ and realized in the local church at the Eucharist. These ministries are not simply an organization established by Christ which the Church is called to preserve, they are the functions of an eschatological anticipation. In Ignatius, Irenaeus, and also Cyprian, the *episkopos* is not an apostle, but the one who, in each church, presides over the Eucharist, sits on that chair which is Christ's chair, holds the Petrine function of proclaiming the true faith (Mt 16:16-18) and strengthening the brethren (Lk 22:32). Reflecting Christ's image, he is also the only shepherd and the only high priest.

These episcopal functions are, of course, inseparable from the retrospective faithfulness to the apostolic kerygma, but they are *made real* within the Pentecostal mystery of the Church, invoking the Spirit, the "other Comforter" promised by Christ. They not only represent apostolic continuity, but also anticipate the final and universal liturgy described in Revelation. Such is the very nature of the sacrament: to anticipate what the Church already is—the Kingdom of God.

Historically, there does not seem to be any other reason

---

[26]"Apostolic Continuity and Orthodox Theology: Towards a Synthesis of Two Perspectives," *St. Vladimir's Theological Quarterly* 19 (1975) 2:83.

for the universal acceptance of what is—rather improperly—called "monarchical episcopate." Apostolic succession alone, it is generally understood today (as an uninterrupted succession going back to the apostles), cannot justify the existence of one bishop in each local church. It is the eschatological dimension of the Eucharist which makes it unavoidable.[27]

Such an eschatological perspective actually provides the necessary safeguard against legalistic institutionalism in ecclesiology. The Spirit bestows upon the bishops a "certain charisma of truth" (*charisma veritatis certum*),[28] but He never becomes prisoner of an institution, or the personal monopoly of any human being. "Where the Church is," writes St. Irenaeus again, "there is the Spirit of God; and where the Spirit of God is, there is the Church, and every kind of grace; but the Spirit is Truth."[29] It is not the Church which, through the medium of its institutions, bestows the Spirit, but it is the Spirit which validates every aspect of Church life, including the institutions. The role of the Church is not to impose upon man a truth which he is incapable of perceiving otherwise, but to restore him in the life of the Spirit, so that he himself might know the Truth.

The Church therefore is an eschatological milieu—the temple of the Spirit—which conditions the existence of a *magisterium,* but no magisterial institution, in itself, can condition the Church. Thus, at all times—and particularly in the Christian East—there was always a recognition that the Spirit can speak not only through the bishops but also indeed through prophets and saints. Sectarian, charismatic trends have often overstated the case for this prophetic leadership. Against such abuses some criteria of authenticity had to be applied; these criteria, however, were not in the ecclesiastical institutions per se, but rather the sacramental framework of the Catholic Church. The true saint or prophet can speak only through the same Spirit: that Spirit which seals the Eucharist.

---

[27]On this issue, see J. Meyendorff, *Orthodoxy and Catholicity* (New York: Sheed and Ward, 1966) pp. 1-16.

[28]Irenaeus, *Against Heresies* 4, 26, 2; ed. cit., *Sources chrétiennes,* 100 (Paris: Cerf, 1965) p. 718.

[29]*Against Heresies* 3, 24, 1; ed. cit. p. 472.

Because the theology of the Spirit is inevitably "apophatic" and paradoxical, the greatest danger is to reduce it to one of its particular aspects only. Such reductions are unfortunately common in the history of ecumenical discussions and dialogues. Much too often such dialogues have attempted to single out external criteria and norms of ecclesiality—the "historic episcopate," the "Roman magisterium," or even creeds, understood as conceptual formulae. The norms, as they exist in the various Christian churches or groups, are then compared and some formal consensus is reached on individual issues. It appears to me that true Christian unity can come about only when Christians join in a common commitment to the One Church, in its historic and, most importantly, eschatological dimensions. The goal is to become this One Church, and through the power of the One Spirit be able to say together, "Come, Lord Jesus!"

CHAPTER II

Greek Philosophy and Christian Theology in the Early Church*

Christianity was born through the ministry of a Jewish Messiah, whose death and resurrection were understood by His disciples as the fulfillment of the biblical prophecies, making Zion a focal point for the salvation of the world as a whole. The authenticity of the Christian message was, therefore, inseparable from its biblical, historical, and Jewish background, but its effectiveness and universality depended upon the way it was transmitted, interpreted, and understood throughout the entire world.

The problem of the relationship between Christianity and Hellenism is, therefore, not simply a matter of comparison between two cultures or two systems of thought: the early Christian community understood its relationship with the Greek world as a *mission* whose success or failure was a test of true universality.

An illustration of this can be seen already in the fact that the "apostolic" writings, which eventually entered the New Testament canon, were written in Greek, although the authors' native tongue was Aramaic or Hebrew. This concern for spreading the Good News about Jesus of Nazareth in the common international language of the times did not imply a renunciation of the biblical roots of the new message. For

*Lecture given on June 1, 1983, at the Orthodox Center of the Ecumenical Patriarchate, Chambésy, Switzerland.

Paul to remain a "Jew," from the seed of Abraham (2 Cor 11:22) was essential to the integrity of his faith, but to become "all things to all men" (1 Cor 9:22) was an inevitable condition of his ministry, because the gospel for which he was responsible was addressed to all. Similarly, the Johannine theology of the Logos, in its basic content, was undoubtedly of Jewish and biblical origin, but could the Evangelist and his readers have used the "Logos" terminology being unaware of its importance in Greek philosophy?

Of course, this missionary universalism was not adopted by all. The existence of a conservative Judeo-Christian tradition was acknowledged in its distinctiveness by the apostolic council in Jerusalem (Acts 15), so that Peter was entrusted with "the gospel to the circumcised" (Gal 2:7). This tradition has survived for centuries in Syriac- or Aramaic-speaking circles. Our contemporary search for the roots of Christianity can discover in it the most primitive expressions of the Christian faith, sometime (but not always) leading to the original apostolic preaching.[1] It cannot be denied, however, that historically this Semitic Christianity developed in somewhat sectarian forms: extreme asceticism and practical withdrawal from missionary responsibility. The remarkable missionary expansion of Syrian monasticism and of the Nestorian catholicossate of Seleucia-Ktesiphon may seem to belie this judgment, but one must remember that it occurred after the adoption of the Nicaean faith and therefore implied a substantial "hellenization." In general, it is the adoption of the Greek language and the use of cultural and philosophical features borrowed from Hellenism which really witnessed to a "catholic" understanding of the Church. Of course Hellenism involved great temptations and led many to erroneous doctrines —which could be corrected only by a return to the biblical (and therefore Jewish) categories of thought—but the Christian gospel had to be proclaimed in a world which spoke and thought in Greek. To do so was not a betrayal of Scripture for a Christian theologian—as Adolf Harnack thought—

[1]Cf. for example the extremely suggestive and important recent book by Robert Murray, *Symbols of Church and Kingdom: A Study of the Early Syrian Tradition* (Cambridge, 1975).

but a direct missionary duty, which was begun by the first generation of Christians and fulfilled by those whom we call "the Fathers."

To address the Greek-speaking and Latin-speaking worlds —including the Roman authorities which persecuted Christians—was the task adopted by those whom we call "the Apologists." Most of the authors generally classified under that label lived in the second and third centuries, but the mental attitude which they represented continued to exist in the writings of major authors of the fourth, fifth, and even sixth centuries. Indeed, until the reign of Justinian (527-580), both in the East and in the West pagan Hellenism represented a spiritual force based on the cultural conservatism of some and the continuous intellectual appeal of Neoplatonism. Like the Apologists of the pre-Constantinian era, many Christian theologians were preoccupied with refuting those neoplatonic positions which they considered incompatible with Christian orthodoxy. Their polemics led them to assume positions which helped establish a continuity between Hellenism and Christianity and thus facilitated the conversion of the last pagan intellectuals.

It is this intellectual and spiritual attitude which alone can explain the appearance in the late fifth century of the extraordinary corpus of writings whose mysterious author used the pseudonym of St. Dionysius the Areopagite.

This paper cannot pretend to discuss all the problems connected with this long period of inner conflict—and also intellectual cross-fertilization—between Hellenism and Christianity. Thus, in the first part I have decided to focus attention on the two major personalities, rightly considered as the real founders of theology in the East and the West respectively: Origen and St. Augustine. Although separated by more than a century of momentous historical events and living under different political conditions, the cultural and philosophical challenge which they faced was finally the same. It was the challenge to "do theology" in a world which had adopted Neoplatonism as its basic philosophy. Their failures and their achievements would have long-lasting consequences in the later centuries.

1. *Origen and Augustine*

It is easy to establish a contrast between their respective historical fates. Origen's thought, even during his lifetime, was the subject of much controversy, and was finally condemned as heretical by the Fifth Ecumenical Council (553). St. Augustine, on the contrary, enjoyed wide respect within Catholic Christianity, was invited to attend the Council of Ephesus (431) and is venerated as a Father of the Church.

But the parallels are no less striking: Origen is so much the real founder of Greek Christian theology that almost no doctrine of God, of Christ, or of salvation, formulated in Greek throughout the following three centuries, can be understood without reference to his system, which as "system" was rejected by the Fathers, but which nevertheless continued to provide them with their terminology, their methods of biblical exegesis, and their principles of spirituality. The influence of Augustine upon the Latin West is even more overwhelming. Until the emergence of early medieval Scholasticism, he is the uncontested and absolute authority in all fields of theology and "has had a greater influence upon the history of dogma and upon religious thought and sentiment in Western Christendom than any other writer outside the canon of Scripture."[2]

This towering importance of Origen and Augustine is of direct relevance to the subject of this paper. Indeed, each of these two exemplary Christians—Origen, a confessor of the faith, and Augustine, mystic and bishop—saw Greek philosophy as the normal intellectual vehicle for the promotion of Christianity and for such an explanation of Christian dogma as was likely to be accepted by their contemporaries. In the case of Origen, the initial, and basically apologetic, concern seems to have been in the field of exegesis: how could Christian Scriptures, written in Hebrew or in poor Greek by authors belonging to an obscure barbarian nation, compete with the really superior achievement of Greek *paideia?* Of

[2]David Knowles, *The Evolution of Medieval Thought* (New York: Vintage Books, 1962) p. 32.

what importance, in terms of the ultimate Truth of existence, were the rudimentary myths of Semitic peoples, the bloody conflicts between obscure chieftains of Palestine, or even the messianic hopes of the Jewish prophets? Origen sought a way in which educated Greeks could read the Old Testament and he found a solution in a "spiritual" understanding of Scripture, which took the form of his famous allegorism. To us the method often appears utterly artificial, but Origen's own preoccupation was in matching the Greek—essentially platonic —intuition that only *eternal truths* really matter, and that therefore the historical events described in Scripture were nothing but figures or parables pointing at fixed and immovable realities, accessible to the mind alone. History did not matter by itself, but only as a pointer towards the eternal world of the Spirit.

As an apology for Christianity, Origen's method proved to be an extraordinary missionary success. Under his influence generations of Greeks accepted the cultural humiliation of having to look for Truth in Jewish Scriptures. We will see below how the great Fathers of the fourth century succeeded in transforming the meaning of Origen's exegetical approach, but the method itself—shorn only of its most obvious excentricities—was preserved by them. It appears not only in patristic commentaries on Scripture, but also in the liturgical tradition of Orthodox Byzantium, which remains the basis of Orthodox spirituality today.

But, as the reader of Origen's most famous systematic *opus* can easily see, the exegetical approach of the great Alexandrian was based on metaphysical presuppositions borrowed from the neoplatonic tradition. According to this tradition, the wisdom and justice of God require that all things be created equal and equally close to God Himself. This implies that God created only equal and identical "spirits" or "minds," made to contemplate the divine essence itself. If the world, as we see it, is full of materiality, diversity, and inequality, this is the consequence of the Fall. Hence, the main goal of Christian life and spirituality lies in restoring unity between the created "mind" and God. Thus, the disciples of Origen—particularly the great Evagrius Ponticus

—formulated the tradition of the constant "prayer of the mind," that foundation of Eastern monastic spiritual discipline and mysticism.

Was this decisive impact of Origen upon both theology and spirituality connected with his use of neoplatonic categories of thought and expression? Unquestionably. How else could he have taught the Greeks to think and to pray as Christians, except by using their language and those elements of their world-view which he considered compatible with the Christian faith? But, of course, he also made major mistakes in his attempts at reconciliation between "Athens" and "Jerusalem." These will be corrected by the Church. But his basic missionary thrust will be assumed and developed in the patristic tradition.

The position of St. Augustine in the Church is, as we said above, quite different, but, like Origen's, his goal is to establish a harmony between faith and philosophical discourse. The famous formula which he used in his *Sermon 43* says it all: *Intellige ut credas, crede ut intelligas* ("In order to believe you must understand, and in order to understand you must believe"). And his method of "understanding" is always based on Neoplatonism. Indeed, it is the reading of Neoplatonists (in Latin translation) which liberated his mind from Manichean dualism, that rational view of reality which he held in his younger, pre-Christian years. Platonic monism was then seen by him as essentially compatible with the biblical view of the one Creator-God, and "in consequence, on almost all points where Scripture gave no lead, Augustine accepted from the *Timaeus* and *Meno* of Plato, and the *Enneads* of Plotinus the explanations they gave of the intellectual problems that engaged his attention, and if a reader of Augustine is in doubt as to the origin of a particular philosophical idea, he will usually find the answer in Plotinus."[3]

There is no way, for example, of understanding St. Augus-

---

[3]Knowles, *Medieval Thought,* p. 36. E. Gilson also characterized the thought of Augustine as "an effort of the Christian faith which seeks to understand its own content, as deeply as possible, with the help of a philosophical technique, which borrows from neoplatonism, and particularly Plotinus" (*La philosophie au Moyen-Age* [Paris, 1952] p. 128).

tine's anthropology and, indeed, his doctrine of God, without referring to neoplatonic categories of thought. His well-known doctrine of knowledge is formulated in terms of an understanding of man as a soul living within a body: it is the soul alone, not the senses of the body, which is able to perceive *permanent* realities and, being itself created—and therefore not "permanent"—it alone understands the difference between transient, created existence and God, the only Absolute. Thus, his theory of knowledge, based on neoplatonic notions, leads Augustine to his doctrine of God. In his early writings he even formally acknowledges that the biblical doctrine of the Creator is the same as "what Plato and Plotinus have said about God."[4] This implies the identification of God as an immutable Essence, both transcendent in its immutability and perceivable in its transcendence by the mutable, created mind: "He who is God is the only unchangeable substance or essence, to whom being itself (from which the noun 'essence' comes) most especially and truly belongs."[5]

Expressed in neoplatonic language, this doctrine, in the mind of St. Augustine, was supposed to express the biblical idea of divine sovereignty, which was implied in the Augustinian understanding of grace and even of predestination. God the Creator is the sovereign God of grace.

It is a matter of controversy whether Augustine's insensibility to the concept of created human freedom—which has really no place in the face of divine grace—is rooted in his Platonism, or whether it comes more exclusively from reading passages in Romans. But it is unquestionable that his doctrine of God, which implies the absolute priority of the Unique Essence over the *personal* or trinitarian aspect of the divine being, comes from his basic philosophic ontology.

So Origen and Augustine, the two founders of speculative theology in the East and in the West respectively, did indeed "hellenize" Christianity. Their intention, as we said earlier, was apologetic and missionary, but the result of their systemizations was to create a problem of orthodox integrity. Is

[4] *Soliloquies* 1, 4, 9; *PL* 32, col. 874.
[5] *On the Trinity* 5, 2, 3; *Corpus Christianorum, Series latina,* Turnhout, 50, 160.

"hellenized Christianity" still Christian? Indeed, on some basic issues of theology and anthropology, Christianity and Platonism were utterly incompatible. In order to become authentically Christian, Hellenism had to be transfigured or "baptized." This process of this transfiguration must be looked for in the later history of patristic thought.

2. The Transfiguration of Hellenism

In the case of St. Augustine, this transfiguration was, in part, occurring through his own personal spiritual odyssey. The Christian authenticity of his conversion, of his famous *Confessions*, of his sermons, and of his activities as a bishop, clearly demonstrate that, whether as a philosopher or as a churchman, he never had any other goal than to be a witness to the gospel of Christ. Furthermore, his definition of God as supreme essence is mitigated by his attempt to use the biblical doctrine of the image of God in man, which is the basis of his so-called "psychological" models of the Trinity. On the other hand, his stand against the heresies of the day—Manicheism, Pelagianism—were recognized as decisive by the Church as a whole.

Nevertheless, it cannot be denied that the intellectual legacy of Augustine—especially in the light of the Orthodox tradition—is somewhat ambiguous. The ambiguity is connected with the fact that his philosophical synthesis was accepted quite uncritically in Western Christianity until the beginning of the great Scholastic era. St. Augustine had no competitor and his writings—which touched on practically every aspect of Church life—were used for centuries in Latin Christendom as a kind of authoritative encyclopedia—a function which the author himself hardly envisaged for them. This is how his concepts of nature and grace, his view on human sexuality, and, perhaps more importantly, his concept of God as supreme essence (which continued to obscure trinitarianism) carried with them forms of unredeemed or untransfigured Platonism (or sometimes Manicheism) which played a role in the gradual theological estrangement between

East and West. St. Augustine himself never envisaged "Augustinism" as a closed and all-encompassing system, but history made it such when cultural differences and institutional conflicts prevented conciliarity and mutual criticism from functioning normally between East and West.

The thought of Origen in the East—unlike that of Augustine in the West—faced challenge from the very beginning. But controversy did not prevent the best theological minds of the fourth century—the Cappadocian Fathers—from using his writings and his ideas; and, later, until the formal condemnation of Origenism by the Fifth Ecumenical Council in 553, a semiclandestine but influential group of predominantly monastic followers of Origen considered themselves to be possessing the ultimate solution of all major theological questions, including christology. This popularity of Origen occasionally took a sectarian character, and can only be explained by the extraordinary congeniality of Origenism with the hellenistic mind. Origen symbolized the possibility for an educated Greek to be also a Christian and provided answers on practically every issue of apparent conflict between Greek philosophy and the Christian faith.

Several of Origen's theological intuitions were adopted as the very foundations of the Greek patristic tradition, although, as we shall see below, their neoplatonic context was radically transformed. For instance, Origen had affirmed that human life is perfectly realized only in the act of contemplation and communion with God: "deification," or *theosis,* is not therefore a divine reality *added to* "nature," but is the realization of an authentic "connaturality" (συγγένεια)[6] between the spiritual side of man and God. This approach excludes opposition between "nature" and "grace"—in the sense in which it was developed in Augustinism—and provides the biblical doctrine of the "image" of God in man with all its spiritual dynamism, so well developed by St. Gregory of Nyssa and St. Maximus the Confessor. Similarly, the major contribution made by the Cappadocian fathers of the fourth century to the trinitarian controversy—the doctrine of the three hypostases in God—has been borrowed primarily from Origen, who was

[6]*On the First Principles* 4, 36.

the first to use Heb 1:3 (the Son as χαρακτὴρ τῆς ὑπο-
στάσεως of God) to generalize the designation of the
persons of the Trinity as *hypostases*.[7] Origen's trinitarian
subordinationism—especially after the Arian misinterpreta-
tion—had to be corrected, but the doctrine of God formulated
in "tri-hypostatic" terms would serve as the main argument
against Sabellian modalism.

Such were the achievements of Origen's thought which
entered the mainstream of Greek patristic thought. But never-
less hellenistic, neoplatonic ideas forming the basis of his
system—in anthropology as well as in the doctrine of God—
required the tests of Christian baptism.

Origen believed and taught that God had created all the
souls (or "minds," νόες) from all eternity, that their connection with bodies was the result of the Fall, and that their
salvation was in a return to an immaterial contemplation of
the divine essence. This basically neoplatonic conception was
incompatible with the Christian doctrines of creation, of
bodily resurrection, and of divine transcendence.

In his authentically biblical understanding of human being,
the great St. Irenaeus had clearly perceived that creatures,
which exist by the will of God, could not be "naturally"
immortal, since God "alone has immortality" (1 Tim 6:16).
Consequently, "the soul participates in life because God wills
it to live; thus it will not even have such participation when
God no longer wills it to live."[8] It remains, however, that not
only Origen but the great Fathers and, indeed, the liturgical
texts frequently refer to the soul as being "immortal." It is
enough to remind ourselves of the well-known dialogue of
St. Gregory of Nyssa with his (and St. Basil's) beloved sister
Macrina *On the Soul and the Resurrection*. The direct influence of Origen on Gregory is undeniable, but there was also
a change of emphasis, well defined by Jaroslav Pelikan: "The
[platonic] idea of the immortality of the soul eventually came
to be identified with the biblical doctrine of the resurrection
of the body, a doctrine one of whose original polemical

---

[7]Cf. particularly *Against Celsus* 8, 12. See G. L. Prestige, *God in Patristic Thought* (London, SPCK, 1952) p. 179.

[8]*Against Heresies* 2, 34, 4.

targets was the immortality of the soul."[9] This convergence of two anthropologies, originally quite incompatible was made possible through the *Christian doctrine of creation.* On this point the Fathers—even those among them who had, like St. Gregory of Nyssa, the greatest admiration for Origen— abandoned him and affirmed (at least implicitly) with St. Irenaeus that the immortality of the soul is not "natural," but is a gift of God to His creatures, anticipating the universal resurrection. It is not linked—as it was in Origen—with the notion of pre-existence of the soul or its eternal creation. It could therefore be harmonized with the doctrine of resurrection. Nothing better than this example shows the inner transformation of Platonism by the acceptance of the biblical doctrine of creation, implying the intervention of a personal and transcendent God in *time,* an idea totally incompatible with any form of platonic speculation. The soul is immortal, but its immortality is *conditional,* always dependent upon the sovereign will of God. It is contingent not only upon the first act of creation itself, but also upon the New Creation, inaugurated in the Incarnation.

Furthermore, anyone recognizing the doctrines of creation and incarnation as decisive for a Christian understanding of man, inevitably accepts the doctrine of a God both trinitarian and transcendent. The reason why the Cappadocian Fathers adopted the origenistic terminology of the three *hypostases* of God—taking the risk of being accused of "tritheism" and subordinationism—is that they intended to express the faith of St. Peter, recognizing the divine identity of the person of Jesus, as the first and fundamental Christian experience. The incarnate Son of God is the God of Christians, not the transcendent Essence of the philosophers. It is at this point that the doctrine of God found in the Cappadocians differs not only from the eternal Creator of Origen, but also from the Absolute Being of Augustine. And the difference can be ultimately reduced to the opposition between "the God of the philosophers and the servants" and the God of Abraham,

[9] *The Christian Tradition: A History of the Development of Doctrine,* vol. 1: *The Emergence of the Catholic Tradition (100-600)* (Chicago: University of Chicago Press, 1971) p. 51.

Isaac, and Jacob. The difference will become even more striking during the christological debates, when St. Cyril of Alexandria will insist upon his famous "theopaschite" formula:
"One of the Holy Trinity suffered in the flesh." The notion
of the impassible, changeless Absolute of Platonism is then
made definitively useless in Christian theology.

This does not mean, however, that the idea of divine
transcendence is abandoned as such. Quite the contrary. It is
Hellenism (and Origen) which believed that the divine
essence itself can be contemplated by the purified mind. The
Cappadocians and the whole Byzantine Orthodox tradition
which depends on them (and on St. Cyril) affirmed the absolute transcendence of the divine *essence,* whereas union with
creation occurs in the *hypostasis* of the Incarnate Logos and
is communicated to those who are "in Christ" through the
divine *energies* which penetrate His deified humanity.

All these are undoubtedly Greek words and Greek concepts, but adapted to the requirements of Christian experience
and Christian theology. And this adaptation is not simply a
verbal adjustment but a radical change and transformation of
the hellenic mind. One can be quite assured that neither Plato
nor Aristotle nor Plotinus would have admitted the legitimacy
of this patristic usage. The confrontation between the Academy
and the Gospel ended with the reality of Christian Hellenism,
not hellenized Christianity.

3. *Byzantium and Hellenism*

The reign of Justinian (527-565) marked the final demise
of hellenic paganism within the Empire: the remaining pagan
schools—including the Academy of Athens—and temples were
closed, and the formal need for "dialogue" with a hostile
pagan world disappeared. It is possible that the author of the
famous *Corpus Areopagiticum,* whose writings were first used
in 533 at a conference in Chalcedon, was the last major
"apologist" of Christianity, addressing himself to neoplatonic
intellectuals. It is also under Justinian that Origen was con-

demned, not only in some of his particular views, but in the very structure of his thought as it approached man and his destiny. It did appear, therefore, that Byzantine orthodoxy was finally eliminating Hellenism, as a danger and a temptation.

Nevertheless, not only was the hellenic world-view still alive through the writings of ps.-Dionysius—which were universally accepted as an authentic witness of an eminent disciple of St. Paul—but the patristic and conciliar formulations of the trinitarian and christological dogmas bore the indelible mark of the doctrinal struggles of the fourth and fifth centuries. And these struggles had been fought not only for the Christian gospel as such, but for its proper interpretation and expression in terms adopted from Greek philosophy, i.e., such terms as "being" (τὸ εἶναι), "essence" (οὐσία), "nature" (φύσις), "substance" or "person" (ὑπόστασις), "energy" (ἐνέργεια), etc. As we saw earlier, the meaning of these terms had been transformed: they acquired in Orthodox theology a dimension and a context which was foreign to Plato, Aristotle, or Plotinus. The words themselves remained Greek, but were now sanctified by patristic and conciliar usage. Their Christian meaning—but also, inevitably, their philosophical history and background—were now inseparable from Holy Tradition.

Furthermore, the writings of the Apologists, whose main point was to assert that Christ was not only the fulfillment of the Old Testament prophets but also of everything that was authentic and true in Greek philosophy, were never disavowed by the Church. St. Basil himself had composed the famous little *Exhortation to Youths as to How They Shall Best Profit by the Writings of Pagan Authors,* and positive references to philosophers—side by side with affirmations of Christian biblical identity—are found in most major Greek and Latin patristic authors.

It is true, however, that throughout the entire history of medieval Byzantine Orthodox thought, the relationship between Greek philosophy and Christian theology never found a universally accepted and peaceful harmony. The classical and somewhat rigid proclamations of Orthodoxy which became common after Justinian, and particularly after the victory over iconoclasm in 843, always associated Plato and Aristotle with paganism. It seems that, precisely because they spoke Greek, the Byzantines were aware—more than the medieval Latins, who had discovered Aristotle in translations from Arabic—of their own pagan past and therefore of the necessity to "baptize" Hellenism before applying it to Christian theology. Even the Mother of God, in the famous, sixth-century hymn "Akathistos" was praised for having shamed the philosophers:

Χαῖρε, φιλοσόφους ἀσόφους δεικνύουσα· χαῖρε, τεχνολόγους ἀλόγους ἐλέγχουσα.
Χαῖρε, ὅτι ἐμωράνθησαν οἱ δεινοὶ συζητηταί· χαῖρε, ὅτι ἐμαράνθησαν οἱ τῶν μύθων ποιηταί.
Χαῖρε, τῶν Ἀθηναίων τὰς πλοκὰς διασπῶσα· χαῖρε, τῶν ἁλιέων τὰς σαγήνας πληροῦσα.

Hail, for you showed that philosophers were foolish; hail, for you made wise men speechless.
Hail, for you confused the inquisitive minds; hail, for you dried up the inventors of myths.
Hail, for you ripped the Athenians' meshes; hail, for you filled the Fishermen's nets.

Similarly, the *Synodikon of Orthodoxy,* read every year on the first Sunday of Lent, anathematized those who, in pursuing "hellenic studies," adopted their "foolish opinions," and those who considered that "the ideas of Plato were true."[10]

This attitude of the Church, so fiercely defensive against Greek philosophy, was supported by the vast majority of Byzantine monastics. This negative attitude of the monks was resented by the scholarly élite, the learned humanists who contributed much to our own modern civilization by preserving and copying the works of ancient pagan authors. However, in each collision between monks and humanists—particularly in the eleventh and fourteenth centuries—victory

[10]*Triodion* (Athens, 1958) pp. 157-58; crit. ed., J. Gouillard, "Le Synodikon de l'Orthodoxie," *Travaux et Mémoires,* 2 (Paris, 1967) pp. 57-59.

went to the monastic party. These were not—as is often thought—victories of obscurantism. The interest in Greek antiquitly was not forcibly suppressed, but its usefulness for theological formulations and problematics was seen as no longer necessary.

In this respect, the contrast between the Byzantine East and the Latin medieval West is really striking. The West, after having been schooled for centuries in the writings of St. Augustine—whose dependence upon Platonism was never fully challenged or redeemed—"discovered" Aristotle in the twelfth century and recognized *him* as "the Master" (*didascalus*). The resulting new synthesis between Greek philosophy and the Christian faith was that of Thomism and medieval Scholasticism in general. This synthesis was not provoked—as that of the Greek Fathers of the fourth century—by apologetic and missionary requirements: it was a purely creative and speculative process (*fides quaerens intellectum*), an attempt to integrate Christianity within a rational system. Since the methodology of this creative synthesis was borrowed from Greek philosophy, it was natural that, on the eve of Byzantium's fall, some Byzantine humanists discovered it as the true fulfillment of the hellenic mind, which now, in their opinion, had no future in the monastically dominated East, but which still held a chance in the Latin West. Thus Demetrios Kydones could complain around 1347 that "because we [the Byzantines] did not care for our own [Greek] wisdom, we considered Latin reasonings to be Latin inventions . . . [for the Latins] show great thirst for walking in those labyrinths of Aristotle and Plato, for which our people never showed interest."[11] Even philosophically oriented defenders of Orthodoxy, like Gennadios Scholarios, express emotional conviction that St. Thomas Aquinas was, in fact, "Greek" in spirit: "O excellent Thomas," he exclaims, "why did heaven give you birth in the West? [If you had been born in the East], you would not have defended the deviations of the Western Church on the procession of the Holy Spirit and on the

---

[11]*Apology 1,* in G. Mercati, *Notizie di Procoro e Demetrio Cidone,* Studi e texti, 56 (Vatican, 1931) p. 366.

distinction between the essence of God and His energy, and you would be our impeccable master in doctrine."[12]

It is an extraordinary discovery that one makes in a comparative study of East and West, that the Greek-speaking and Greek-thinking Orthodox Byzantium was much more consistently aware of the incompatibilities between ancient Greek philosophy and the gospel than was the Latin West. Indeed, Demetrios Kydones and Gennadios Scholarios were, in fact, isolated and nostalgic intellectuals: it is not in them that Orthodoxy recognized itself, but in the great monastic theologians, whose witness and whose insistence on the "one thing needful" preserved the tradition throughout tragic and culturally-dark times.

Conclusion: Catholicity and Tradition

"The Church is apostolic indeed, but the Church is also patristic," wrote Father Georges Florovsky[13] to show that there is no way in which one can remain faithful to the original gospel without learning how the Fathers defended it, and without sharing in their struggle to formulate it in a way accessible to their contemporaries. Indeed, it is *their* victory over heresies that the Church endorsed at its ecumenical councils. They are "Fathers" because the Church recognized them— and not their adversaries—as having taken the right positions on issues of faith. And, as I pointed out earlier, these issues arose in the painful process of the conversion of the Greek world to Christianity, as the Fathers, being themselves culturally a part of that world, were trying to make the transition easier and, therefore, being as welcoming as they could to the terms, the concepts, and the legitimate intuitions of Greek philosophy. Actually, in this process they were witnessing to the authentic *catholicity* of the Church, its mission to all, its responsibility for saving the world, and its ability to

[12]G. Scholarios, *Oeuvres complètes,* eds. L. Petit and M. Jugie (Paris, 1928-36) vol. 6, p. 1.
[13]*Bible, Church, Tradition: An Eastern Orthodox View* (Belmont, Mass.: Nordland, 1972) p. 107.

assume and bless whatever is worth saving, especially when that assumption leads to the salvation of many.

In what sense, therefore, is the Church "patristic"?

On the one hand, it is committed to the truth which the Fathers preserved in their struggles, and there is no way in which that truth can be known and understood except by entering the "mind" of the Fathers, becoming their contemporaries in spirit and, therefore, allowing oneself to become as Greek as they were. Our theology today must maintain *consistency* with their positions: all Orthodox theologians must therefore become "Greek" in that sense.

On the other hand, the Church catholic is called today to save not the Greeks of the past, but men and women of the twentieth century. Being "patristic" therefore does not mean that one simply repeats their formulae and their ideas: indeed, *consistency*—i.e., the true the true content of Holy Tradition —is not identical with repetition. Faithfulness to the Fathers— who spoke to Greeks and converted the Greeks to the great truths of the gospel—requires that we speak to our contemporaries and convert *them.*

But this missionary responsibility of the Church catholic is meaningless unless one perceives within its entire history— starting with its apostolic foundation and continuing through its great encounter with the thought of ancient Greece—the same living Truth, a Truth which saves all the cultures and all the civilizations which are able—as Greek wisdom was in the persons of the Fathers—to transform themselves within the baptismal font.

CHAPTER III

Church and Ministry*

For an Orthodox-Lutheran Dialogue

The history of Christianity is rarely envisaged in a global —or "catholic"—perspective. The Reformation in particular is most often studied in the light of its immediate roots in Western Christendom, as a reaction against medieval Latin structures, against the papacy in particular, and anticipated in the Conciliarism of the early fifteenth century. An Orthodox historian, however, is bound to look at the momentous events of the sixteenth century in the light of the even earlier and, for him more fundamental, rupture which split the Christian world in two halves: Eastern Orthodoxy and Roman Catholicism. And when he adopts this wider—and for him quite natural—perspective, he recognizes inevitably that Martin Luther and the other Reformers were not in direct conflict with the Orthodox Church, but with a papacy which had earlier been seen in the East as being somewhat in conflict withe Christian message. The Reformation then appears to him as a consequence of the original schism between East and West.

Today, attempting to rebuild Christian unity, we look for a possibility to reverse the process of separation. In the light of this new approach, the schisms of the past often acquire a

*Lecture given at the theological convocation on Ministry and Polity, Lutheran School of Theology, Chicago, Ill., Feb. 7, 1983, and also published in *Dialog,* 22, Spring, 1983, pp. 114-120.

new historical dimension: that of lost opportunities, which can and should serve as lessons for the future. Obviously, the opportunity in the sixteenth century was lost because of the absence of the Orthodox East in the tragic struggle within Western Christendom. I believe that it is possible to make this affirmation without indulging in simplistic Orthodox triumphalism, but simply by recognizing that the Reformers faced and rejected a Catholic tradition which in their time had already lost its original balance.

Actually, the Reformers were not completely oblivious of the Christian tradition of the East, and used its witness in their antipapal polemics. Luther himself appeals to the "Greeks"—in conjunction with the Bohemian Hussites—as being more faithful to the gospel than the Romanists, e.g. in their eucharistic practice.[1] More significant still is the prolonged effort of Melanchton and other Tübingen theologians to establish contacts with Patriarch Jeremiah II of Constantinople (1573-1581).[2] However, at that time East and West lived in different worlds, not only politically and culturally but also spiritually and intellectually. The contacts could not really jell into a significant dialogue. Both Romans and Reformers tried to use the East in their polemics against each other, while the East itself remained passively frozen within the tight framework of the Muslim occupation of the Middle East, or, in Russia, in a state of cultural infancy, having only recently emerged from the Mongol conquest.

What is sad, however, is that the opportunity missed in the sixteenth century has not yet been picked up in our time. Throughout the nineteenth century relations between Lutherans and Orthodox in Eastern Europe were largely dominated by the ethnic and cultural constituency of each tradition— Germanic on the one side, Slavic on the other—and were

[1]"Pagan Servitude of the Church," in *Martin Luther: Selections from His Writings,* ed., John Dillenberger, (Garden City, NJ: Anchor Books, 1961) pp. 261-62.

[2]Most accessible edition of the Greek version in I. Karmiris, Τὰ δογματικὰ καὶ συμβολικὰ μνημεῖα τῆς ὀρθοδόξου καθολικῆς ἐκκλησίας, I-II, (Athens, 1952) pp. 375-489. German text and commentary in *Wort und Mysterium. Dokumente der Orthodoxen Kirchen zur ökumenischen Frage,* II. Herausgegeben von Aussenamt der Evangelischen Kirche in Deutschland (Written, Luther-Verlag, 1958).

limited to academic encounters. In the twentieth century, in spite of the worldwide ecumenical movement, the academic and ecclesiastico-political dimensions of existing dialogues have never been really transcended. Even in the United States the very traditionalism of both the Lutherans and the Orthodox tends to reduce contacts to a level not very different from that which existed in Europe.

However, as Lutheranism is now overcoming the limitations of immigrant history and defining its confessional and ecclesial unity within the realities of American society, and as Orthodoxy also begins to move in the same direction, the true, in-depth encounter becomes inevitable. We speak the same language, our young people go to the same schools, and we all face the same divided, secular, and disoriented world, seeking Christ's justice and truth. It is, therefore, less likely than before that cultural reasons will remain decisive in perpetuating misunderstandings between us. These reasons have lost their *raison d'être*.

Clearly, history itself and, indeed, the Lord of history call us to the *basics* of the Christian faith: can we or can we not confess them together, and what would be the implications of such a common confession?

In a sense, this indispensable return to the "basics" makes it easier for me to approach the topic of the ministry, for indeed I believe that the problem cannot be solved within the categories and concepts used during the Reformation-Counter-Reformation struggle, but must be based upon a fresh reading of the New Testament and the early Christian tradition.

1. *The Origins of the Episcopal Ministry*

As a collection of writings composed on different occasions, by different people, and for different immediate purposes, the New Testament does not use a consistent terminology on the issue of the ministry. Furthermore, the conditions under which the Christian communities existed in the apostolic age were different from ours. This is why the simple use of proof-texts, as has been so often done since the sixteenth century to make one point or another in the debate between Reformers and Counter-Reformers, has generally led to dead ends.

However, while Jesus did not leave the Christian communities with detailed institutional directives, the extraordinary fact remains that by the middle of the second century there existed a uniform pattern of church structure, adopted by all local churches. This basic unity—which did not exclude some diversity in forms—can be explained either by an unlikely, extra-Christian influence decisive enough to be universally accepted without controversy, or *by the very nature of the Church herself.*

It is my strong belief that the latter is indeed the case and that, therefore, the present-day ecumenical debate about the ministry is not a matter of pure historical research, but fundamentally a debate on ecclesiology. What we are after is not a ministry, mutually recognized by several otherwise separated denominations holding different interpretations of the New Testament data and diverse views on the Church, but a consciousness of belonging to the One Church of Christ and an agreement on what this Church is in her very being. Once this inner consciousness and agreement are recognized it is, of course, possible to speak of formal imperfections in the empirical life of the Church and its ministries, and also of legitimate diversities, which existed already in apostolic times and are still inevitable today. But a recognition of basic unity should precede acknowledgment of diversity. Such an understanding of the ecumenical debate may seem utopian, but in my opinion it alone can lead to true unity.

Formal or descriptive evidence concerning the life of the Christian communities in the first century is extremely scarce. It can be affirmed, however, that the fundamental spiritual realities were for these communities an *anamnesis* or "remembrance" of the death and resurrection of Jesus as saving events, and an *eschatological* anticipation of the coming of His Kingdom. This anamnesis and this anticipation were both realized in the eucharistic meal: "For as often as you eat this bread and drink this cup, you proclaim the Lord's death until

He comes" (1 Cor 11:26). It was in the eucharistic meal and through it that the Church was truly herself, the Church of God (ἐκκλησία Θεοῦ), and it is, therefore, within the framework of the eucharistic assembly, gathered every week on the Lord's Day, that the internal structure of the Church had to take its shape.[3] Indeed, if the Eucharist was a reenactment of the Last Supper, someone had to sit in the place of the Lord and pronounce the words He commanded His disciples to say. On the other hand, the Eucharist was also a participation in the forthcoming Messianic banquet of the Kingdom as it was seen by the author of Revelation: "a throne stood in heaven, with One seated on the throne . . . Round the throne were twenty-four thrones, and seated on the thrones were twenty-four elders [*presbyteroi*] . . ." (4:2, 4).

There is no doubt that when Ignatius of Antioch, who was martyred under Trajan (A.D. 98-117), was describing a local Christian community and comparing the bishop with the Father and the presbyters with the apostolic college (*Trall.* 3:1), he had precisely this vision of church order, based not on some legal transmission of powers from Christ through the apostles to the bishops, but rather upon the

---

[3]The method which consists in looking into the original sacramental nature of the Church for the real origin of Church structure has been developed by the Orthodox theologian N. Afanassieff (see particularly *Tserkov Dukha Svyatogo* [Paris: YMCA Press, 1971]; also "L'Eglise qui préside dans l'amour," in N. Afanassieff, et al., *La Primauté de Pierre dans l'Eglise Orthodoxe* [Neuchâtel, 1960] pp. 9-64). The name of Afanassieff is therefore attached to what is generally called "eucharistic ecclesiology." There is no doubt that the thought of Afanassieff was influenced by Rudolf Sohm's opposition between the Spirit and the Law in understanding the structure of the early Church, and therefore in discovering continuity not in legally defined institutionalism, but in "spiritual" consistency. The works of Sohm were quite popular among Russian theologians before the Revolution (see the Russian translation of Sohm's *Kirchenrecht* [Leipzig, 1892] by the famous Paul Florensky in cooperation with A. Petrovsky, Moscow, 1906). However, Sohm's charismaticism received in Afanassieff the correction of sacramentalism. More recently, and independently, the centrality of the Eucharist for the understanding of the early Church and for the solving of contemporary ecclesiological problems is developed by John Zizioulas (see particularly, "Apostolic Continuity and Orthodox Theology: Towards a Synthesis of Two Perspectives," *St. Vladimir's Theological Quarterly* 19 [1975] 2:75-108; *L'Etre ecclésial* [Geneva: Labor et Fides, 1981]). See also J. Meyendorff, *Orthodoxy and Catholicity* (New York: Sheed and Ward, 1966) pp. 1-16.

nature of the local eucharistic community: "Get close to your bishop," he writes, ". . . that is how unity and harmony come to prevail. Make no mistake about it: if anyone is not inside the sanctuary, he lacks God's bread" (*Eph.* 5:1-2). The connection is clearly established between "unity and harmony," i.e., between essential qualities of the Church and the functions of the bishop within the eucharistic assembly. Indeed, "you should regard that Eucharist as valid which is celebrated either by the bishop or by someone he authorizes. Where the bishop is present, there let the congregation gather, just as where Jesus Christ is, there is the Catholic Church" (*Smyrn.* 8:1-2). Similar quotations from Ignatius, familiar to most students of the early Church, could be easily multiplied. Sometimes historians have interpreted them as showing the author to be a revolutionary reformer, establishing a new ministry— the "monarchical episcopate"—in a church which had inherited a much more diversified ministry from apostolic times. But nothing in Ignatius supports the idea that he was a revolutionary. He writes as if his correspondents were fully familiar with the episcopal ministry, and we know of no adverse reaction from any quarter against his vision of church structure. That structure became the standard model everywhere. No scheme is able to explain the existence and the general acceptance of the "Ignatian" episcopate in the early second century more convincingly than the sacramental or eucharistic approach to early Christian ecclesiology. This approach was not invented by Ignatius but was rooted in the very nature of the early Christian communities.

The New Testament writings use a variety of terms to designate the leadership of the Christian churches. The terms *episkopos* and *presbyteros* in particular are used interchangeably and apply to the entire body of elders which, in the churches founded by Paul, exercised functions of leadership in each local church. However, the Pauline epistles also mention "presidents" (προϊστάμενοι)—"those over you in the Lord," προϊστάμενοι ὑμῶν ἐν Κυρίῳ (see 1 Thess 5:12)— a title which refers to those who preside at the eucharistic assembly. Moreover, in the pastoral epistles, the function of "presidency" (προϊστᾶναι) begins to be definitely associated with that of *episkopos* (1 Tim 3:4-5; 5:17). The role played by the apostle Peter as head of the original community in Jerusalem, and his succession in the person of James, provided a personalized—"monarchical"—image of the later "episcopal" ministry. As Peter together with the apostles led the church in Jerusalem, so James, after Peter's departure, headed it together with presbyters. The model of the church of Jerusalem, in its "anamnetic" and its eschatological dimensions, was in fact necessarily a model for New Israel everywhere. Thus, in Ignatius the "presbyters" around the bishop represent the senate of the apostles. Also, quite importantly, not only in pre-Constantinian patristic literature (especially Cyprian), but also in the medieval Byzantine authors, Peter was always seen as the prototype of the bishop in each local church.[4]

The term "catholic church" applies in Ignatius—and in all contemporary sources—to the local eucharistic community: each church is, indeed, ἐκκλησία Θεοῦ in its fullness, because what gives that fullness is God's presence, is the Body of Christ indivisibly manifested in each Eucharist. This understanding of catholicity, however, is not congregationalism; catholicity implies unity with the past (apostolicity) and with the future (eschatology), and also unity in faith and life with all the other churches which share the same catholicity. Local churches are identical in their faith, and therefore always interdependent. Although celebrated locally, the Eucharist has a cosmic or universal significance. The Church is always the same Church of God, although she sojourns (παροικοῦσα) in different geographic locations.

The unity with the past is a unity in the faith "once delivered to the saints" through Christ's witnesses, the apostles. Hence, "apostolic succession" is a succession in the faith of the apostles, witnessed in the continuity of the Eucharist. It is not simply a continuity in beliefs or in convictions; the faith is taught within the Eucharist; it is there also that it is being received and maintained by the entire people of God, by the power of the Spirit. It is this concep-

[4]Cf. texts gathered in J. Meyendorff, "St. Peter in Byzantine Theology," in *The Primacy of Peter in the Orthodox Church* (London: Faith Press, 1963).

tion of apostolic tradition that Irenaeus, in the second half of the second century, opposed to the secret or esoteric conception of tradition held by the Gnostics.

On the other hand, the link with the apostolic past presupposes unity in space between the local churches. This unity is manifested in the *identity* of their apostolic faith, also well described by Irenaeus. No local church possesses the exclusive privilege of preserving apostolicity, although, in fact, some churches did enjoy more favorable historical conditions and received particular *charismata*. These special gifts were then used to help others, and were to be "received" or recognized as such by all the other churches. After the third century, the most normal way of maintaining and manifesting unity in faith was found in the councils of bishops who, together with the people, defined the faith which was then "received" by those churches which were not represented at a given council. In this process, the guiding principle was always obedience to the Spirit of God, not to majority opinion established by democratic vote.

These basic principles of early Christian ecclesiology provide a framework for contemporary discussion. I referred to them because they contain both the limitations and the potential of possible dialogue leading to an eventual, mutual recognition between churches which have been separated for centuries and are now called to recognize each other again within the same Christian faith.

2. *Orthodox Attitudes in History*

One of the most obvious and most important conclusions provided by the evidence coming from the early Church is that a "recognition" of orders or ministries is not simply a recognition of ministries as such, but of the *church* in which these ministries are exercised, and of the *faith* held by that church. It is interesting to note that the schisms of the third and later centuries led to prolonged discussion as to whether the baptism of heretics or schismatics was to be recognized. The issue of the ministries was treated almost as an afterthought. The central problem was whether the Novatians, the Donatists, the various categories of Gnostics, and the later heretics could or could not baptize and thus add new members to the One Church. A community using a recognizable baptism would necessarily be considered as possessing a recognizable ministry: sacraments and faith were seen as inseparable.

In practice, no really consistent attitude was ever formulated. In his *Letter 188*, St. Basil of Caesarea, after writing several paragraphs setting forth his rejection of the Encratite baptism, surprisingly adds:

> But I know that we have received the brethren Izois and Saturninus into episcopal rank, who were of that party. Therefore we can no longer separate from the Church those who have joined their company, since through the acceptance of the bishops we have published a kind of canon of communion with them.[5]

Historically, we know practically nothing of Izois and Saturninus, but the somewhat paradoxical attitude of St. Basil towards them and towards the issue of reconciliation with dissident communities clearly shows that the real issue was whether such communities could be considered as *churches* or not. It is on the basis of that decision that the particular —and pastoral—issues of baptism and the ministries can also be solved.

It can be shown, I think, that Basil's attitude represented a model for later generations. The evidence of an *agreement in faith* between local churches was the necessary sign of, and the condition for, church union. In the late fourth century, for example, the reunion between the Nicaeans and those who, in the East, were reluctant to accept Nicaea for terminological reasons (and who represented a majority of those who were at various times considered "Arians"), occurred by an agreement in faith, followed by sacramental communion. Before such formal, corporate reunion occurred, individuals were accepted either through baptism or through

[5]Saint Basil, *The Letters*, trans. R. J. Deferrari III (Cambridge, MA: Harvard University Press, 1962) pp. 20-21.

annointment with chrism or through simple confession of
faith (cf. Trullan Council, A.D. 692, canon 95). The matter
of ministries was never debated per se, and its resolution
came each time in the context of a complete agreement in
faith between churches.

Throughout the centuries there have been variations in
the practical policies of the Orthodox Church in matters of
reunion with non-Orthodox Christians,[6] but, behind these
practical inconsistencies (which have parallels in the history
of Western Christendom) there was ecclesiological continuity: *the faith* remained as the ultimate sign of "apostolic
tradition," expressed particularly in the episcopal ministry
but also in other basic components of the canonical, sacramental, and liturgical tradition.

This consistency of the Orthodox vis-à-vis a different
approach to episcopacy within the Anglican communion manifested itself clearly in the various conversations and statements concerned with Anglican orders between World War I
and World War II. Throughout those conversations the
Anglicans were particularly, if not exclusively, concerned
with having their orders "recognized as valid" on the basis
of an uninterrupted chain of consecrations going back to the
apostles. The Orthodox, on the other hand, while admitting
the existence of such an uninterrupted chain within Anglican-
ism, kept expressing concern for the unity of faith. Some
autocephalous Orthodox Churches favored the acceptance of
Anglican ministers without reordination, but only "in case
of the union of the two churches,"[7] and of course excluding
any intercommunion before full dogmatic unity should be
achieved.[8] Eventually, in 1948 in Moscow, most Orthodox
churches signed an even more negative statement on the issue,
referring to the absence of doctrinal agreement[9] with the
Anglicans.

[6]On this subject see the recent article of Bishop Peter L'Huillier, "The
Reception of Roman Catholics into Orthodoxy: Historical Variations and
Norms," *St. Vladimir's Theological Quarterly* 24 (1980) 2:75-82.
    [7]Statement of Constantinople, July 28, 1922, in E. R. Hardy Jr., *Orthodox
Statements on Anglican Orders* (New York: Morehouse-Gorham, 1946) p. 4.
    [8]Statement of Cyprus, March 7/20, 1923, ibid., p. 9.
    [9]For a more detailed and technical discussion of this issue see *Ministers*

Clearly, the bottom issue in those debates was the refusal of the Orthodox to accept "apostolic succession" (understood as mechanical continuity) as the *only* criterion of ecclesial and sacramentl reality. They always denied that the Church was somehow created simply by the fact of episcopal succession, but rather insisted that true episcopate existed only within the true Church. Apostolic "succession" has no reality outside of apostolic "tradition," and the guardian of apostolic tradition is the whole Church, although the bishops within the Church are its most responsible witnesses. It does seem to me that, on this point, further dialogue with Reformation theologians is both possible and desirable.

3. *The Ministry and the Church Today*

In the history of the modern ecumenical movement no initiative came closer to a full theological and practical approach to this issue than the consensus document on "Baptism, Eucharist and Ministry" worked out by the Commission on Faith and Order of the World Council of Churches. This text is presently under study by all member churches.[10] Certainly, the document does not solve all the problems. It is generally acknowledged, however, that in this particular ecumenical consensus the contribution of the Orthodox members of the Commission has been substantial. One of the most important of such Orthodox contributions is, in my opinion, the *ecclesiological setting* of the document. For instance, it is affirmed that "ordination is an acknowledgement by the Church of the gifts of the Spirit in the one ordained, and a commitment by both the Church and the ordained to the new relationship" (par. 44). The necessary consequence of this *ecclesial* character of ordination—an act of the whole Church and not simply the passing on of some powers from one individual to another—lies in the concluding paragraph of the document concerned with an eventual "mutual recog-

---

of Christ, ed. Th. O. Wedel (New York, Seabury, 1964), especially my article, "The Bishop in the Church," pp. 150-65.

[10]*Faith and Order Paper No. 111*, (Geneva: WCC, 1982) 33 pp.

nition." This "mutual recognition" would not be a simple recognition of "ministries," but a mutual recognition of *churches*: "The mutual recognition *of churches and their ministries* implies decision by the appropriate authorities and a liturgical act, from which point unity would be publicly manifest . . . The common celebration of the Eucharist would certainly be the place for such an act" (par. 55, italics mine).

It is at this point that the reason for the Orthodox objections against any form of *inter*-communion between yet divided churches becomes apparent. In such inter-communion there is an unavoidable lack of true, mutual commitment to catholic unity, and a peculiar reduction of the sacramental reality either to a mechanistic act of bestowing grace, or to pietism. Within such a reduced catholicity there cannot be any mutual recognition of ministries. The Orthodox, in their rejection of inter-communion, are often accused of stubborn confessionalism. It would be fairer to recognize in their attitude on this particular point an authentic concern for true catholic unity and a reluctance to accept substitutes for it.

Actually, such mechanistic or pietistic reductionism in medieval Christianity was vehemently objected to by Martin Luther,[11] who opposed to it his understanding of the faith as a response to the Word of God, being also confessed in the sacraments. Between the Orthodox and the Lutherans, therefore, the real issues are the content and the implications of that faith, and particularly whether the sacraments involve a sacramental *structure* of the Church herself, whether this basic structure goes back to the apostolic witness, and what are its permanent, unchangeable elements. But there is a common starting point: the apostolic succession of the ministry is not an institution above the Church but a part of the *apostolic tradition* which is a continuity in the apostolic faith,

---

[11]There is also a remarkable, clear criticism of such reductions in Gustaf Aulen's *The Faith of the Christian Church*, trans. from the fifth Swedish edition by Eric H. Wahlstrom (Philadelphia: Fortress Press, 1960) pp. 366-68. On the positive side, Orthodox theologians often find themselves at home with the re-emerging tradition of sacramentalism and patristic scholarship within Lutheranism; e.g., G. L. C. Frank, "A Lutheran Turned Eastwards: The Use of the Greek Fathers in the Eucharistic Theology of Martin Chemnitz," *St. Vladimir's Theological Quarterly* 26 (1982) 3:155-71.

held by the people of God, and sealed by the gifts of the Holy Spirit, promised by the Lord for His Church.[12]

If one accepts the principle that the unity of separated Christians can only be achieved through their recognition of each other as members of the One Church, and if that unity itself is indeed to be described as an inner sense, an inner commitment—spiritual, doctrinal, sacramental, institutional —to the One Church, then the entire theological methodology of the ecumenical quest begins to transcend the simple comparison of conceptual, doctrinal statements. In that sense, it seems quite important for us today to overcome that particular form of confessionalism which emerged in Europe after the Reformation. I mean here the definition of church membership by the acceptance of this or that historical confessional formulation (Augsburg, Westminster, etc.). The Church Catholic is never bound by such historical "symbols." The councils of the early Church never produced exhaustive "confessions," but rather condemned individuals or doctrines which were seen as incompatible with the Apostolic Tradition. The Apostolic Truth itself was always considered to be inexhaustible in human words. The Catholic Church holds that living faith which is expressed in the Scriptures and maintained by Tradition. The goal of ecumenism should be the recovering of that experience of a common faith.

In America, confessionalism further evolved into "denominationalism," where church membership is in fact defined by even more mundane categories: ethnic background, social status, etc., even if *pro forma* reference is also made to doctrinal traditions.

It seems to me that the present trend towards unity within American Lutheranism, resulting from the coming merger of two denominations into a united new church, can become a really significant event of Christian reintegration if, by transcending both denominationalism and confessionalism, it moves in the direction of a renewed church-consciousness. However, from an Orthodox viewpoint, there is also a danger that in reaction to the somewhat sectarian confessionalism of

[12]Cf. the definition of "apostolic succession" as "succession in the apostolic tradition," in "Baptism, Eucharist and Ministry," part IV, par. 34-35.

those Lutherans who stay outside of the union, i.e. the Missouri and the Wisconsin synods, the new church will, on the contrary, evolve towards the relativistic denominational-ism of "broad" Protestantism.

The Church can never be a "denomination" or a "confession." Her "being" is not determined by accidental historical events or situations, but the *hapax*-event of Christ's death and resurrection, and by the *coming* Kingdom. This is why catholicity is possible only within the apostolic faith (because the apostles witnessed to the Resurrection) and in expectation of the eschatological fulfillment. In order to be authentically "catholic," one must transcend—or at least be free from—the contingency of the present by accepting the acts of God, both past and forthcoming. This looks like a little impractical, but catholicity transcends practicality, as it must also transcend history, geography, and culture. It is fully manifested only in the Eucharist, which is, as we have seen earlier, both a memorial and an anticipation. But this transcendent nature of the Church's being is also liberating: the good news of the Resurrection of Christ liberates humanity from historical, geographic, or rational determinism. It makes us free by faith.

The issue of the ministry can therefore be ultimately reduced to the question of whether one defines it as a projection of secular, historical realities, such as power, efficiency, social justice (e.g., equality of the sexes), or as a function within the eucharistic assembly. In the latter case, the ministry is apostolic, unchangeable, and eschatological in nature. The bishop presides at the assembly, as Peter presided over the church of Jerusalem after Pentecost, and as the One sitting on the throne in heaven, described in Revelation (4:2ff).

In practical terms, the Faith and Order document on "Baptism, Eucharist and Ministries" reaches the conclusion that "the threefold ministry of bishop, presbyter and deacon may serve today as an expression of the unity we seek and also as a means for achieving it" (par. 22). However, it also recognizes that "churches maintaining the threefold pattern will need to ask how its potential can be fully developed for the most effective witness of the Church in this world" (par.

25). This is a mild and diplomatic way of raising the question of whether the traditional structure, where it exists, is being used in accordance with its own nature and purpose. Can one say, for example, that the pope and bishops opposed by Luther in the sixteenth century were performing a ministry which was really identical with that described by Ignatius of Antioch? Of course, one may argue that the original functions of the *episkopos,* as head of the local eucharistic community, would be modified with new requirements of the *episkope,* as they emerged after the third century when the bishop began supervising not one but several eucharistic communities. Perhaps this was a necessary development, securing in particular the necessary unity of the local churches on the regional and even the universal levels, a condition for a meaningful Christian witness in the world.

But what about the power structures of feudal or imperial origin which began to be used as standard reference to define episcopal authority? What about the rise of papal primacy? What about purely titular bishops, consecrated without election by or responsibility for a concrete local church? Such questions are indeed applicable not only to the Roman Catholic and Anglican traditions but to the Orthodox as well. They emerge inevitably in the mind of any Protestant conditioned by his own history and observing the historical realities of "catholic" Christianity. How often, instead of transcending history, "catholicity" was—and still is—invoked to justify surrender to worldly categories! The Orthodox theologian might observe in defense of his Church that none of these medieval or post-medieval developments in the exercise of the episcopal ministry were ever elevated to the level of formal doctrinal definition or commitment (as the papacy was in the West), but he will still face great difficulty in presenting the actual realities of contemporary Orthodoxy as unequivocally consistent in practice with those of the early Church.

It is obvious, therefore, that if one is to move in the direction of Christian unity, the issue of the ministries should be approached both in the light of their God-established apostolic origin and in the light of the various ways they have been exercised in history. It is only a fundamental agreement on the nature of the Church, and a common experience of it, which can lead to mutual recognition. Agreement needs critical study of one's own past and present but, first and foremost, a vision, a common discovery of the "realized eschatology" which makes the church to be the Church.

CHAPTER IV

The Significance of the Reformation in the History of Christendom*

Not being a specialist in the history of the Reformation, I am quite unqualified to give a technical historical evaluation of the big crisis of the sixteenth century in the Western part of Christendom. What I shall try to present is a theological interpretation of Protestantism as it can be viewed today by an Orthodox theologian, starting with its origins in the Western Church itself and continuing with the later evolutions of the Reformed movement. Since the principle of *ecclesia reformata et semper reformanda* was, and still is, one of the fundamentals of Protestantism, the Reformation cannot be considered as a single event, chronologically limited to the sixteenth century: it is essentially an *open* movement whose *raison d'être* was and is to *remain* open, to be continually attentive to the Word of God, and to reform itself in accordance with the divine will. It would, therefore, be historically and theologically inaccurate to judge the Reformation only on the basis of what Luther or Calvin said. In order to understand Protestantism fully, it is necessary to investigate what the Western Church, as a whole, was in the sixteenth century, what was the Reformers' essential claim, and what Protestantism, as a whole, later became.

*A talk delivered at a Protestant-Orthodox Consultation in connection with the Faith and Order Conference, Montreal, 1963, and published previously in J. Meyendorff, *Orthodoxy and Catholicity*, New York, 1965, pp. 119-140.

I

In overcoming the Manichean convictions of his youthful years, St. Augustine formulated a philosophical system, inspired mainly by his platonic readings which conceived God as the Supreme Good, origin of all existing beings. This idea appeared to Augustine as the most adequate expression of the biblical God to whom his conversion had led him. It constituted a strong negative safeguard against Manichean dualism, but, at the same time, it led the father of Western Christianity to the identification of God with a rationally conceivable essence, that of the Supreme Good. Instead of having an ontological existence, as was the case in Manicheism, evil became a simple absence of Good, since Good was identical with the absolute and divine original being.

In developing his system, Augustine was, of course, aware of the biblical idea of a God essentially *transcendent*—an idea which found another expression in the apophatic, or negative, theology of the Fathers; but this transcendence of God was, for him, relative to the deficiency of the creature, especially that of the *fallen* creature. God is invisible, incomprehensible, unknowable, because man does not possess the necessary vision to see Him, the necessary intellect to comprehend Him, and the necessary knowledge to know Him. However, with the help of grace, man is able to develop a natural capability to know God. This capability is, for Augustine, the *sensus mentis*—an intellectual sense—which naturally belongs only to the *soul* and which is able to know the essence of God, once the soul is liberated from its present dependence upon the body. A platonizing dualism in anthropology thus takes the place, for Augustine, of his original Manichean ontological dualism.

On the other hand, we know that the Augustinian doctrine of original sin (as opposed, first, to the naturalistic optimism of Pelagius and then proposed against Julian of Eclana as a justification of infant baptism) is based upon the concept of the inherited *guilt* for the sin of Adam. *In quo omnes peccaverunt*: this incorrect Latin translation of Romans

5:12 added a juridicial character to the Augustinian interpretation of original sin and provided additional argument in favor of a juridical understanding of salvation. The New Testament doctrine of justification, which is to be understood in the context of the Pauline concept of the old *Law*—showing the sin to be a sin, but also fulfilled in Christ, in whom we are justified for the Law—is thus taken out of its proper New Testament context, and included in a more general metaphysical frame, overshadowing all the other concepts with which the Bible describes salvation: sanctification, new life, union with God, participation in the divine nature. The *massa damnata* of the fallen humanity is the object of God's wrath because it is *guilty.* It can be justified by *grace* which alone can first *forgive,* then restore man to the natural capability of his soul to contemplate God's essence. The latter can occur only beyond the grave; in the present life, man can never be anything else than a forgiven sinner.

The doctrine of God as the Supreme Good in His essence and the Augustinian doctrine of original sin remained intact in the developments which Augustinianism incurred during the period of Western Scholasticism. However, Thomas Aquinas radically abandoned Augustine's theology of knowledge. The starting point of Thomism is the Aristotelian affirmation that all human knowledge starts with *sensible* experience. There is no innate *sensus mentis* which would be able to lead the intellect to the Supreme Good. Human knowledge consists in the ability of the mind to make sensible objects intelligible, and this, in turn, can lead to a relative and indirect knowledge of God. Direct knowledge about God comes from revelation—the Scripture or the Church's Tradition—which is quite independent from, although not contrary to, reason. The activity of the human mind which is based not on sensible experience but on revealed truths is called "theology." It is a natural activity of the mind and it follows all the rules of intellectual scientific research. As such, it is liable to error, and, in order to remain in the Truth, it needs the guidance of the God-established *magisterium* of the Church. Direct *vision* of the essence of God will, however, be accessible to the elect in the future life.

Salvation, in Scholastic theology, is conceived along Augustinian lines and interpreted in increasingly juridical terms. Anselm's theory of satisfaction, being soon universally accepted, provides an interpretation of Christ's redemptive sacrifice through which we are all justified in the eyes of God. The fruits of this sacrifice are bestowed through grace which first justifies, then creates in us a *state,* or *habitus,* through which our acts or works acquire a *meritorious* character. Grace, therefore, both precedes and accompanies the act of our free will. The Church, which disposes in this world of the gifts of grace, is vicariously empowered to bestow a meritorious character to the acts of our free will; hence her sacramental powers and the practice of indulgences. The tendency to interpret salvation along these lines becomes increasingly prevalent in the late nominalistic developments of Scholasticism.

It is quite unnecessary to speak here in detail about the Reformers' reaction to this Scholastic system. With Luther, it was, first of all, the idea of salvation *sola fide* and *sola gratia* without anything other than the direct power of God's love and the human faith which receives this grace; without any meritorious "works" which would be unable to add anything to Christ's saving gift; without all those magical acts, often bought for money and allegedly providing automatic but limited and individual graces. To all the "means of salvation," too cheap and human, offered to the Christian by the medieval Western Church, Luther opposed the absolute powerlessness of fallen man (which was also felt by Augustine) and the power of the *gospel.* It is precisely to this powerlessness that the gospel gives an answer. Man cannot save himself; another one saves him. That is why man has to *believe* in this Other One.

Thus Luther's main intention was to go back to the New Testament, to revive the sense of the God of the Bible, the living God, the Creator and the Sovereign. He recovers the primitive concept of salvation, as a *drama,* a *battle* between God and the evil powers of death and sin which have usurped God's sovereignty over the world. As Aulèn has shown in *Christus Victor,* Lutheran theology was indeed a reestablishment of the basic biblical and patristic elements in this drama. His concern for the catholic tradition of the Church was obvious, and the Augsburg Confession itself claims to be nothing else than a reestablishment of the ancient apostolic faith liberated from all human philosophical systems. Lutheranism also recovers the sense of mystery of God, revealed *yet* unknown (*revelatus et absconditus*). It is historically probable that Luther was directly inspired by the Rhenish mystics of the fourteenth century, Eckhardt and Tauler, but it is even more significant that he frequently refers also to Chrysostom's treatise *On the Incomprehensibility of God*. And this preoccupation and feeling of the mystery of God did not disappear when the "prophetic" Reformation of Luther took, with Calvin, the aspect of a strict system. The whole *religion* of Calvin resides precisely in a mystical contemplation of this mystery: *Soli deo gloria*. The negations of the Reformers are all directed against ideas and institutions which seem to deprive God of the worship and the glory due to Him alone. When Scholasticism presented the traditions and dogmas of the Church as rational developments of revealed statements sanctioned by the *magisterium*, the Reformers rejected these dogmas and these traditions precisely as human and rational and therefore never to be identified with the Word of God. The gulf between faith and reason, between God and fallen human nature, which was inherited from Augustine, maintained in Thomism, and even widened in the Nominalist Scholasticism of Occam, remained as the common denominator of Western Christianity before and after the Reformation. Rome maintained, however, that God remains present in the created world *vicariously*, through the *authority* of the Church which He Himself created for this purpose, through *created grace*—the created *habitus* of Thomism—which grants to the actions of human free will a meritorious character and, therefore, renders human sainthood possible. The Reformers rejected this created grace altogether as an idolatrous corruption of Christianity: God is God, and man is a sinner. In order to justify man, God does not need man's cooperation; man cannot have any "merit" in the face of God. God speaks, man listens; God forgives, man receives forgiveness through faith. God saves whom He wants to save and condemns those who are predestinated for damnation. And we have seen that the foundations of this lucid Calvinistic logic were laid by Augustine.

The later developments of Reformed Christendom are related to these original presuppositions. Scripture, as Word of God, was opposed from the beginnings of the Reformation to the words of man. However, the nineteenth century witnessed the development of biblical criticism: Protestant scholars discovered and Protestant theologians realized that the Bible was very much a *human* document. In fact, the nucleus of this problem was already in Luther's critical attitude toward the "straw epistle" of James. In any case, modern biblical criticism brought about a real revolution in a large part of Protestantism. The Word of God is no more in the letter of the Bible, but only in the nucleus of an original kerygma which is being defined in various ways and precludes any divine intervention in the normal, natural stage of created beings. Thus, one comes to a kind of thoroughly demythologized deism, extremely remote from the main intuition of the Reformers which was to make a *living* God freely and immediately present to man.

Of course, several phenomena in the history of Protestantism do not exactly fit in this broad picture. I have in mind, for example, the eighteenth-century German pietism, or the Wesleyan fresh approach to the New Testament. But, generally speaking, these movements retained their freshness —and, I would say, their ecumenical significance—only as long as they were not conceptualized and made part of the main stream of Protestant theology. Once integrated into that stream, their influence was *ipso facto* restricted to the realm of "piety," "emotionalism."

II

In the East the relations of God and man are conceived by the Greek Fathers differently than in the line of thought which started with Augustine.

On the one hand, the distinction between the Creator and the creature is maintained with full strength, especially since Athanasius: divine essence and human nature can *never* mix or be confounded or be participated by each other. God is *absolutely* transcendent in this essence, which can never be known or seen even in the life to come. The divine transcendence is not due, as in Augustine, to the limitations of our fallen state or to the imperfections of our bodily existence, disappearing when our soul is liberated from material bonds: God, in His very being, is *above* creature; He is always free in His relation with the created world, and nothing created can either possess Him or see Him. The whole negative (or apophatic) theology of the Fathers expresses precisely this and reflects the fundamental biblical view of the transcendent God.

However, the existence of man, as a creature of God, is not viewed as a *closed* existence: man has been created in order to share in the life of God, in order to be *with* God. The Genesis story of the establishment of man as king and ruler of the universe speaks precisely of that: God does not create on earth a viceroy or a vicar, but a being who shares in *His* own properties, who rules not "in the *name* of God," but *in God*, and who, first of all, shares in a quality which belongs properly to God alone: immortality. In other words, what makes man to be a man, and not a beast, is his faculty, originally established by God, to share in God's immortality, in God's power over creatures, and even in God's creative power. One can immediately see here that the problem of grace and nature are conceived quite differently from the Augustinian tradition: grace is not a created gift, given as a *donum superadditum* to an otherwise perfect and immortal being. It is the divine life itself given to man who has been *created in order* to receive it and to share in it and who, if he is deprived of grace, ceases to be consistent with *his own* nature. Man, therefore, is conceived dynamically not only in what he is—a creature—but also in what he is called to be, "partakers of the divine nature" (2 Pet 1:4).

And, of course, God is not identified with the static idea of the Supreme Good. Absolutely transcendent in His essence,

He is an acting, living God. He is not limited by any of the human concepts which can be applied to Him. One cannot say only that He *is* the Good: He is, but He is also above all the good that a created mind can conceive. He is both transcendent *and* immanent, because He *wants* to communicate Himself to the creature and He wants the creature to share in His own faculties. In fact, the Reformers were quite close to that notion in their idea of *Deus revelatus qua absconditus,* but the whole intellectual tradition to which they belonged prevented them from drawing further conclusions. In the East, especially since the fourth century, it was common teaching that in God essence is to be distinguished from "acts" or "energies," that the transcendence of God is not a prison in which He is secluded, that He is not only free to reveal Himself and to communicate His life, but that He created man precisely in order to have him share in His divine immortality and joy.

The fall of man consisted in man's preference to compete with God, to be His equal instead of participating in His gifts. As a result, he abandoned his own destiny, the proper aim of his nature, and became enslaved to the power of death because he did not possess immortality as a property of his own. There is no question, in patristic theology, of an inherited guilt transmitted to the human race through the sin of Adam. What is inherited by the entire human nature is slavery to death and corruption. Luther was restoring the classical patristic idea (which is reaffirmed, every Sunday, by the Byzantine liturgical texts) that the drama of the Fall and of salvation was played not in an abstract, juridical, utilitarian manner between God's justice and man's transgressions, but that it involved three sides: God, man, and the Devil. Instead of the Augustinian idea of the inherited guilt—only personal sins can produce guilt—the Fathers spoke of a *personal* power of death and corruption, that of the Devil, from which Christ came to liberate man, "trampling down death by death."

In Christ, indeed, man is given justification before God's law. But he is also restored into the fellowship of God and the participation in divine life: the original relationships between God and man are not only reestablished, but, since

God Himself has become man, one is allowed to say, with Irenaeus and Athanasius, that man is becoming God. The "deification" of man, this central point in patristic doctrine of salvation, is, of course, suspected in the West of being a single transposition of neoplatonic pantheism. But it would be this only if one held to a much more Greek idea of God as a simple essence. In fact, in patristic theology the deification of man preserves the absolute transcendence of God and His absolute freedom: He *gives* us His own life. In receiving it, man does not "possess" God, he does not become God in essence; he participates in that which is given to him and thanks God for His ineffable grace. This grace is not a created *habitus* which would give a meritorious character to human acts; it is God Himself who acts in man's own salvation.

Augustine's and Calvin's concern for always affirming the unique sovereignty of God and the sufficiency of His grace is obviously met here. However, their refusal to admit any human meritorious participation in the act of salvation is simply out of place. There is no question of *adding* human acts to the divine act, which otherwise would be insufficient for man's salvation. The whole problem is not a juridical and utilitarian one—what is sufficient, and what is not—but rather a question of the original human destiny, which is to be *with* God and *in* God.

This original human destiny has been restored in Christ, the New Adam. He was perfectly God in His divine nature and His divine will, and perfectly and authentically man in His human nature and His human will. In His divine hypostasis the gulf created by the Fall between God and man has been bridged forever, and in Him we have again access to the Father and become participants in the divine nature. What He is by nature, we become by grace.

No Orthodox theologian will consider that all this is only a Chalcedonian or post-Chalcedonian development of Eastern religious thought; he will read these fundamental experiences of the Orthodox sacramental and liturgical life on practically every page of the New Testament. It is necessary to keep this in mind in order to understand the Orthodox reaction before the historical fact of the Reformation.

Already in the last century the Russian publicist and theologian, A. S. Khomiakov, noticed that the movement of the Reformation stopped at the frontiers of the Orthodox world, even after it had deeply penetrated into countries like Moravia and Poland which were Roman Catholic. This does not mean, of course, that the historical Christian East was free from all internal diseases capable of provoking dramatic schisms. After the fifth century, the Eastern Church was torn apart by the christological issue, and the schism between the Orthodox Dyophysites (or Chalcedonians) and the Monophysite or Nestorian communities of the East has not yet been healed. In later times the Russian Old Believers seceded on ritualistic issues, and even today the Eastern Church is being torn apart by similar movements, such as the Greek Old-Calendarists. Mystical sects were always numerous in Russia, but they were never able to attract significant masses of the Orthodox population of the country. In the nineteenth and twentieth centuries more or less significant bodies of Protestants, mainly Presbyterian or Baptist, appeared both in Russia and in the Middle East. But, whatever can be said of their spiritual vitality—and there is no doubt that there is a lot of vitality in the modern Russian Baptist movement—it cannot be denied that these groups are a pure importation from the West and not a product of the local religious tradition. To see this, it is sufficient to consult their devotional liturgical books which are, for the most part, translations of Western hymns. And whatever their future may be, it will be related to the general disappearance today of the cultural and historical barriers between East and West. This disappearance has in itself a great ecumenical importance, as we shall try to show a little later, but does not necessarily solve the theological problem which divides East and West as spiritual entities.

The historical impermeability of the Orthodox world to the great movement of the Reformation simply illustrates the fact that the theological formulation of Protestantism—at least when it is seen in the light of Eastern patristic tradition—is fundamentallyy dependent upon Western Augustinian problematics. However, when one considers some of the essential religious intuitions of the Reformers, one is struck by their convergence with the most important elements of the patristic synthesis. I am thinking now, in particular, of the idea that saving grace can never, under any circumstances, be considered as *created*. This was, in fact, the main intuition of both Luther and Calvin when they rejected created, meritorious *media* between God and man and also the created institutions which were supposed to "administer" or "dispense" God's grace. There is undoubtedly a fundamental encounter between them and Orthodoxy, where neither the idea of created grace nor that of a human "merit" for man's salvation can find any place. This encounter is simply based on a common understanding of the gospel of Christ liberated from all philosophical reinterpretations.

Why then, if they are so clearly united on the *Soli Deo Gloria,* do Orthodoxy and Protestantism so widely diverge on such issues as sacramental theology, veneration of the Virgin Mary and the saints, and ecclesiology? It seems to me that an Orthodox theologian is not able to pass a judgment on the matter without considering the Western Augustinian tradition taken *as a whole.* It is from this tradition that there comes the idea that God, being identical with His essence, cannot be *participated* otherwise than in His essence. Since participation in the essence of God—being admitted in the *visio beatifica* of the Scholastics—is irreconcilable with the transcendentalism of the Reformed theology, it is clear that no real *participation* in God is possible. But it is only such a participation which justifies, in Orthodoxy, both veneration of saints and sacramental realism. On the other hand, the patristic view of *man* as being *created in order to share in God's life,* in order to be *active* in accordance with his own destiny as determined by God, excludes the purely passive role of man in his own salvation. Christ has two natures and two wills, but the actor is *one,* acting in a divine-human *synergy.* In Christ, our will is active, but in a redeemed, new manner; it does not only "receive," it acts, but not in order to fulfil a "requirement" which would have been left unfulfilled by

God; our will acts in Christ in order to fulfil in itself the
image of the Creator which was obscured by the Fall but
which has been restored in Jesus to its former beauty.

There is no doubt that the Reformation was a great movement of liberation from false categories imprisoning the
Christian gospel. But in rejecting the doctrines and the institutions which were considered as created intermediaries of
grace, the Reformers—it seems—were unaware of a christology
and an ecclesiology other than the Augustinian and the
scholastic. An Orthodox theologian can say, therefore, that
they rejected not the catholic tradition of the Church, but its
one-sided and corrupt form. They were undoubtedly looking
for this authentic, true tradition and, in several instances,
were practically on the verge of identifying it in the same
terms as does the Orthodox Church. In addition to the several
instances that we have already noted, the idea of *Ecclesia
reformata et semper reformanda* is obviously a Protestant
form of understanding Tradition. The principle of the
"Church reformed and always to be reformed" can and must
be applied, in Orthodoxy, to those elements which are only
human, and they are many in the historical Church. Moreover,
that which *God gives to us,* the divine presence of His fullness in us and among us, in the sacraments and in the Truth
preserved by the Holy Spirit in the Church, is above and
beyond "reformation." It can be either accepted or refused.
Orthodox and Protestants can certainly agree on the principle
of a permanent reformation of that which is human in the
Church; where we differ, as I have tried to show, is in the
extent to which the human is being *assumed* by God and
deified, on the principle of the intrinsic communion between
God and man in the Church.

The historical circumstances of the sixteenth century,
which continued until modern times, prevented any real contact between Reformed Christendom and Orthodoxy. Those
historical circumstances should always serve as a reminder
to the Orthodox of the fact that the Church must not only
be Orthodox and Catholic through the gift of God, but also
look Catholic and Orthodox in the eyes of others. Would the
development of Western Christendom not be quite different

if there had been some Orthodox *presence* in the West during such crucial periods as the Conciliar schisms of the fifteenth century, or the big crisis of the sixteenth? But in those days, the tragic estrangement between East and West had already been an established fact for many years. Seen in the light of what happened in the West throughout the Middle Ages and the Renaissance, the Orthodox historian cannot avoid considering the schism between Rome and Constantinople as the fundamental, the basic tragedy in the history of Christianity through which the whole of the Christian West lost its theological and spiritual balance. The Orthodox East was often led to adopt toward the West an attitude of sufficiency, and this is undoubtedly our—very human—sin: for it belongs to the very essence of catholicity to share in the brother's problems and to help him in resolving them before rushing into anathemas and condemnations. However, it is quite important to remember that, while the West was engaged in a series of dramatic crises—the "big schism," Reformation, Counter-Reformation—Eastern Christendom was concerned with tremendous external catastrophies: the "brotherly" visit of the crusaders in Constantinople in 1204, the Mongol invasion of Russia in the thirteenth century, the Arab conquest of the Middle East and the capture of Constantinople and the Balkan peninsula by the Turks in the fifteenth. All this did not favor theological dialogue and spiritual communication, and thus what the Reformers saw in the East was hardly more than a vestige of the past, whose relevance could only consist in the fact that it was also "non-Roman" Christianity. They showed much good will, however, and were quite ready to listen to the voice of the Eastern Church: this is particularly shown by the personal approaches of Philip Melanchton to Jeremiah II of Constantinople (1555-1565), his letter to the Patriarch, stating that he and the other Reformers accept the teachings of Athanasius, Basil, Gregory, Epiphanius, Theodoret, and Irenaeus. Later the Augsburg Confession was sent in Greek to Patriarch Jeremiah II, and a famous correspondence took place between the Tübingen theologians and the Ecumenical Patriarch. It shows quite clearly the earnest desire of the Reformers to be in communion with the whole universal

Church, of which they considered the Eastern Church to be a part, but it also manifests the absence, in those days, of a real common language. Jeremiah II obviously considered the Protestants as being an internal schism in the West and ignored the substance of the issues which brought them out of the Roman fold. This is shown in the fact that he devotes pages in all three of his letters to the question of the *filioque* which he considers as *the* Western heresy *par excellence,* while giving his approval to the Reformers' doctrine of original sin. Of course, the *filioque* problem does exist and manifests a doctrine of God which is probably at the root of the main theological issues between East and West; but Jeremiah in the sixteenth century was quite unable to build a coordinated view of the problem. His correspondence with the Tübingen theologians simply shows to him that the Reformation was *not* a return to Orthodoxy, and he stopped the dialogue for which he was not prepared.

The seventeenth and the eighteenth centuries were probably the most tragic periods in the history of Orthodox theology. Both in the Middle West and in Russia it underwent what Father Florovsky once called a "Western captivity." While patristic spirituality and theology were preserved in the monasteries, in the liturgical books, and in popular piety, they were practically forgotten by the few educated people whose schooling was necessarily either Roman Catholic or Protestant. The instinctive reaction of the Orthodox Church against the activities of Western missionaries thus took the unavoidable form of using Protestant arguments against Romans and Roman arguments against Protestants. Both the Protestantizing and the Romanizing parties also fought each other inside the Church, while ambassadors of the Roman Catholic powers (France, Austria) and of the Reformed Western states (Holland, Britain) actively intervened in enthroning and dethroning ecumenical patriarchs, using money and political influence at the Sultan's court. Their interest in the Eastern Church was mainly connected with their struggle against each other, each side wishing to have the Orthodox in its own fold. Thus Orthodoxy got involved in the Western disputes not in order to solve them, but in order to be *used* as additional arguments. I am mentioning all these tragic events here simply because they have influenced the historic relation between Protestants and Orthodox until this day, both on a theological and on a psychological level, by giving to each side a certain picture of the other and by establishing certain habits and attitudes which are not easy to modify.

It is in this setting that the case of Cyril Loukaris is to be understood. This interesting man, one of the most educated Greeks of his time, published in 1621 a confession of faith entirely formulated in Calvinistic terms. This case is important for us because it provoked the first historical confessional reaction of Orthodoxy to the Reformation. A turmoil took place throughout the Orthodox Church. Loukaris' confession was condemned by a series of councils (Constantinople, Kiev, Jassy) where, of course, the latinizing tendency prevailed. The so-called "Confession of Dositheos," confirmed by a council in Bethlehem in 1675, is the most important, and also, fortunately, the less Latin manifestation of this reaction, where the "errors of Luther and Calvin" were unmistakenly condemned.

So an encounter took place, but how much of a dialogue? How much of a real understanding of the issues involved? Neither the historical circumstances nor the theological climate permitted then a mutual understanding.

At this point, I draw some general conclusions.

1. Viewing the history of Christendom from the point of view of doctrinal development, an Orthodox theologian necessarily considers the estrangement of East and West since the early Middle Ages as the deepest and most fundamental root of later schisms. This does not mean that all Christian theology should have normally consisted in simply repeating the theology of the Greek Fathers. The question here is not in asking for a mechanical fossilization of *one* particular historical period of tradition; it is a question of *consensus* and *continuity.* An Orthodox believes that there is essential *unity* between the biblical view of God and man and the Greek patristic synthesis, and this is why for him the Fathers are "The Fathers." Each father may have had his own one-sided

views of the mystery of Christ, and he must then be corrected by the *consensus*. St. Augustine himself is at the origin of later Western developments only because he has been isolated from the entire tradition of the Church and considered the unique source of theological knowledge. Thus a new synthesis and a new *consensus* took place. The Orthodox reject this new synthesis not for the sake of its novelty—new theologies, new formulations of doctrine, are not only unavoidable but quite necessary if the Church is truly catholic and wants to send its message to all peoples and all cultures—but because it is incompatible with the understanding of the gospel of Christ as expressed in the Bible and the Fathers. However, the Reformation was indeed an attempt to liberate Western Christianity from the scholastic frame of thought and to draw it back to the Bible and to primitive Christianity. We have tried to show where this attempt seems to us to be incomplete. The total absence of Orthodoxy in the big Western drama, the lack of concern for the Western developments, will certainly be on the Last Day one of the heaviest burdens we shall have to bear facing the Lord's Judgment Seat, although some extenuating circumstances will be found for us in the historical catastrophies in which the Christian East was involved.

2. The Reformation, as a fact in the history of Christendom, cannot be evaluated on the basis of what the Reformers wrote or said. Sometimes it seems almost impossible to identify the various aspects of modern Protestantism as belonging to the same tradition. However, this is only a superficial impression. In both Barth and Bultmann there is the common intuition that the Word of God and the word of man remain *extrinsic* to each other. The development followed by Barth in his later works and leading to a new discovery of the Word of God in the created world, to a solidarity between God and man in the *natural* order—this idea was always strong in the West, both in Thomism and in modern liberalism, and was also stressed by Russian sophiologists. It is still quite different from the notion of a *free* mutual participation of God and man *in the Church* through the Word's historic incarnation. Thus, whether one holds an optimistic anthropology, so wide-

spread in American Protestantism, or the pessimistic Calvinistic remembrance of sin still holding humanity, whether one considers God as the Forgiver or simply as a nice heavenly Father who has nothing to forgive, it remains that the life of the Christian in the Church does not *participate* in God's life. Hence, of course, in both the "neo-Orthodox" and in the "liberal" camp of Protestantism, many hold as indifferent for the essential Christian kerygma whether Christ was God or not, whether His Resurrection was or was not a historical fact. And then one is bound to ask oneself what is left of the biblical and patristic synthesis and of Christianity in general —this Christianity that every Orthodox *does experience* on the practical and "naive" level of Protestant worship and life, if and when they remain in the line of the ancient tradition. For the Orthodox, the essence of the gospel resides precisely in fact that God *does* speak through the human lips of the historical God-man Jesus who rose from the dead; He speaks in the Bible, in tradition, in the sacramental structure of the Church, in the personalities of saints. God *has given us* all this without prejudice to His essential transcendence.

3. My third and final conclusion concerns the Ecumenical Movement. Orthodox ecclesiology is based upon the unity of local churches recognizing in each other the same faith, the same sacramental divine presence, and witnessing to this unity through common action and communion of spiritual life. Schism occurs when this mutual recognition disappears. This happened between the East and the West in the early Middle Ages. The Reformation produced in the West a new situation, but the first superficial attempts made by the Orthodox to recognize in the Reformed communities the same revealed fullness of Christ's truth and presence failed. The Ecumenical Movement is today the continuation of these efforts of recognition. They represent a necessary and absolute condition for communion in faith and sacraments. They bring mutual knowledge, hence their theological and ecclesiological significance, even if—and this does unfortunately happen—they produce disappointment and frustration. Frustration, pain, and suffering are unavoidable whenever there is error and schism until they are cured.

Now, we can ask ourselves, how much mutual knowledge and understanding has been achieved? The least that one can answer is that we are still at the very beginning of the road, if one considers the situation of the two spiritual worlds to which we belong. We have a lot more to do. But on the way it is essential not to get lost in byways. Let us frankly face the issue: Does the present structure of the World Council of Churches reflect the real theological and spiritual situation of the Christian world? How much place is given to the dialogue between Orthodoxy and Protestantism as two entities? It is in such a dialogue that the real issue is to be solved, as we have tried to show. It is not clear, anyhow, that the problem of uniting Methodists and Presbyterians with each other is of a quite different nature from that which confronts the relations between Orthodoxy and Protestantism as a whole. In the present institutional and psychological situation of the World Council of Churches, the Orthodox Church looks as if it were an extreme right wing of non-Roman Christianity, a kind of super-high church, exotic, irrelevant in its solemnity .

The Orthodox themselves are, to a very large extent, responsible for this situation. Their way of being represented in the World Council without the necessary theological preparation and personnel, limiting themselves to separate declarations—obviously necessary in themselves but insufficient to replace a real participation and influence in the ecumenical debate—confuses the isues in the eyes of many. There must be a new stage in our relations.

We are living in a time when many of the old issues can now be more easily clarified. The historical estrangement of East and West—linguistic, spiritual, intellectual—is bound to disappear in a world which becomes too small. The "non-theological" elements of our estrangement will soon belong to the past. Orthodoxy today is no more—and will become less and less—an "Eastern" Church, just as Western Christianity ceases to be only "Western." This will help us to forget the relative issues and concentrate on the real ones. Let us see in all this the hand of God.

CHAPTER V

Does Christian Tradition
Have a Future?*

Our society today is witnessing a remarkable revival of traditionalisms. I use "traditionalism" in the plural, because today's pluralistic and secular society inevitably searches for its *roots* in a variety of ways. The unifying American dream of a new world—pure, Christian and ultimately free from the corruptions of the old—is, of course, still alive, but it is being challenged by innumerable groups searching for their identity elsewhere. Partly inspired by the growth of Black community consciousness, and emulating the revived identity of the Jews, other ethnic groups are being led to assert themselves as separate cultures and traditions. In the past, all these movements would have been considered un-American, and certain conservative elements of American society obviously still look at the "ethnics" with dismay and latent disapproval. However, institutions try to react constructively, and universities encourage ethnic studies. Thus, the idea of cultural pluralism is being integrated in to the American dream itself.

I am referring to these facts only to focus our attention on the contrast between the revival of traditionalism in secular society and the obvious crisis and confusion present in our notions about the *Christian tradition.* We are, in fact, in the

*The Eighth Annual Thomas Verner Moore Lecture, sponsored by St. Anselm's Abbey, and delivered at the Catholic University, Washington, D.C., on September 26, 1981. Published also in *St. Vladimir's Theological Quarterly,* 26 (1982), 3, pp. 139-154.

midst of a crisis of Christian identity. Indeed, any collective identity is inseparable from tradition: one can be a Chinaman, a Jew, or an Irishman only by an association with the past history of the Chinese, the Jews, or the Irish. Similarly, one is a Christian because one identifies first of all with the historical person of Jesus Christ and also with Christians of past ages. But here confusion comes, because of competing interpretations of who Christ was and what He preached, because of divisions among Christians and—specifically in our time—because of a crisis in the institutions whose function it was and still is to teach and maintain the Christian tradition. The result is that secular traditions are readily honored and respected, people die for the preservation of their national and cultural traditions and are venerated as heroes for doing so, but if someone presents himself as a "traditional" Christian, or simply refers to the authority of tradition, he is identified as a conservative who refuses the necessary "updating" of the Christian faith. In a sense, among Christians "tradition" has become a bad word.

The problem lies also in the fact that, in the light of the Christian faith, tradition is not a simple concept. It is certainly not mere respect for the past. This complexity itself has led to reductions and simplifications. It also leads many Christians today into confusing secular and religious traditional values, which eventually reduces Christianity to being a mere external adornment, used by fundamentally secular ideologists of the left or of the right.

In my attempt to discuss these issues—speaking not as a sociologist or a psychologist, but only as a historian and a theologian—I will try first to define tradition not only in terms of the past to be preserved but in terms of the *future* to be anticipated and prepared. Second, I will make a historical excursus into the second century of the Christian era, because at that time the situation of the Church was, in certain extraordinary ways, similar to our own. Finally, I will speak of our present ecumenical situation and touch upon the approaches to the issue as they appear in the three major Christian families—Roman Catholic, Protestant, and Orthodox.

Tradition and Eschatology

As distinct from Platonism and other forms of static philosophical idealism, the Bible reveals the actions of God in history. The world has a beginning and an end, determined by God. Also, the Bible is incompatible with ontological dualism: since God created the world Himself—and not, for example, through the mediation of some inferior demiurge (as the Gnostics used to think)—this world, whether "visible" or "invisible," is good and is destined to salvation. However, the Bible also affirms an existential dualism between "this world," which finds itself in a state of rebellion against its Creator, and "the age to come," when God will be "all in all" (1 Cor 15:28, KJV).

Thus, in this period of time between the beginning and the end, humanity in general, and each human being in particular, is offered the opportunity of reasserting his loyalty toward God and of struggling against the "prince of this world," the "tyrant" or "usurper," who controls creation through the power of death. And the New Testament tells us that, in a sense, man can prepare, anticipate, and even provoke the end; that the end, although fully determined by God, also awaits man's readiness to meet it.

One might ask, perhaps, at this point whether this eschatological approach has anything to do with tradition. Indeed it has, because in the Christian revelation *alpha* and *omega* do coincide, and because life and truth coincide. Without eschatology, traditionalism is turned only to the past: it is nothing but archeology, antiquarianism, conservatism, reaction, refusal of history, escapism. Authentic Christian traditionalism remembers and maintains the past not because it is past, but because it is the only way to meet the future, to become ready for it. Let us recall the meaning of the Christian eucharistic celebration: it is, indeed, a *memorial* of what Jesus did in the past, but it is also performed "until He comes," it is based on the expectation of His coming. In the eucharistic canon of St John Chrysostom, immediately after the words of institution, the Orthodox Church specifically remembers "all those things which have come to pass for us: the Cross, the Tomb, the Resurrection on the third day, the Ascension into heaven, the Sitting at the right hand, and the second and glorious Coming"—as if the Second Coming had already occurred! And the interior design of ancient Christian—both Romanesque and Byzantine—churches always places at the very center an eschatological image: the *Pantokrator,* or the image of an empty throne, prepared for the One who is coming. The Eucharist not only remembers, it also prepares, awaits, and anticipates.

In later centuries, this eschatological dimension was largely forgotten. How many of our modern church buildings reflect it? Who preaches about it? No wonder that a true sense of tradition was also lost.

One should note, however, that even if one were to recover the eschatological content of the Christian faith, it could be understood in different ways. Here are three examples, which are directly relevant for the Christian attitude toward the world and which qualify all aspects of Christian ethics.

(a) Eschatology can turn apocalyptic: *The kingdom of God is coming soon; there is nothing to expect from history; Christians can do nothing to improve human reality; even the smallest social cell—the family—is only a burden and is of no justifiable concern.* The Church here is reduced to a "remnant," which can only appeal for its Lord—"Come, Lord Jesus!" (Rev 22:20). No real mission or responsibility for society or culture is then possible or even desirable. God is seen alone as the Lord of history, acting without any cooperation or *synergia* (cf 1 Cor 3:9). The new Jerusalem is coming from heaven all prepared (Rev 21:2), and we have nothing to contribute to it. It is understandable that sometimes Christians adopt such an apocalyptic eschatology, especially when they find themselves in hostile societies and are deprived by force of any possibility of influencing the world around them. Such was the case of some early Christian communities, and this is reflected in the New Testament itself. Similar situations exist even today, for example, in Communist countries. In such particular, extreme situations, apocalypticism is perhaps legitimate. But clearly, apocalyptic eschatology, since it sees no *future* for Christianity (except the parousia), is not concerned about the past either: it does not admit of any tradition, any culture, any progression or regression in humanity's quest for God. And, of course, it has been rejected by the Church as a *permanent* interpretation of Christian eschatology. Indeed, the Church believes that the "new Jerusalem," the Kingdom to come, is not only a free gift of God but also a seal and a fulfillment of all the positive, creative efforts of mankind to "cooperate" with the Creator throughout the entire process of history. This is why, when the Roman state accepted Christianity, the Church welcomed the opportunity and the responsibility that fell to her, in spite of all the risks and temptations it entailed. Since that time, the idea of Christian tradition has become inseparable from what we call Christian culture.

(b) On the opposite extreme of apocalyptic eschatology stands the humanistic and optimistic understanding of history: the belief that the historical process is controlled by man and that it can and should be understood in a rational theory of progress. In this approach, history indeed has a meaning, and there is also necessarily a place for tradition, which is understood primarily in terms of an interplay between "progressive" and "reactionary" trends. This optimistic belief in progress can be called a "post-Christian" phenomenon (the importance it attributes to history would be difficult to imagine, for example, in a society dominated by a Buddhist set of values). Since the time of the Enlightenment, this optimistic eschatology has been dominant in Western society and, in the twentieth century, has spread even to China in its Marxist form. Whether or not it still calls itself Christian, this type of "eschatology" identifies the new Jerusalem with human achievements, understood in secular terms. Its tragedy resides in its fundamental utopianism. Indeed, it ignores basic realities of human life, such as death and sin, which occur both on a personal and a societal level and cannot be overcome by social progress alone. It conceives of an endless civilization which—if realized— would be as horrible as the eternal survival of a human being dominated by sickness and old age. Accepting the idea that the human person is subject to necessities of historical determinism, it destroys the main content of Christian hope: that Christ's resurrection has liberated man from dependence upon "powers and principalities" ruling in the fallen world, that death has no power, that man is no longer a prisoner of social, physical, or historical conditioning.

Clearly, this eschatology, based on the optimistic idea of human progress and, in fact, suppressing the human freedom of ultimate self-determination, is incompatible with the idea of Christian tradition.

(c) The third type of eschatology is based on the biblical concept of *prophecy*. In both the Old and the New Testaments, the prophet does not simply forecast the future or announce the inevitable. The biblical prophet issues either a promise or a threat. Generally, the two are combined. But prophecy always places man before an option, a choice between two types of personal or social behavior. He is *free* to choose, but the prophet has informed him of the consequences. Such an eschatology has been called *conditional eschatology,* and it constitutes the only theologically acceptable basis for the idea of tradition as well.

Indeed, what we call Holy Tradition is the history of the right choices made by human beings confronted by the prophetic word of God, responding correctly in the concrete historical circumstances of their time. They are those whom we call saints. Accepting tradition actually means to live in the communion of saints, who lived in the past but have also prepared the future. Their correct choices have concerned Christian doctrine or Christian life. We may be living in different historical circumstances, and the options that confront us may not be identical with theirs, but the effort to remain in communion with them is a necessary and crucial element of the Christian faith itself, because that faith is concerned with history. This concern for the "communion of saints" has sometimes also been called "catholicty in time." Without that aspect of catholicity, "catholicty in space"— that is, the external, geographic universality of the Church— has very little meaning. Also, quite importantly, the saints of the past cannot be fully understood by us without our awareness—at least partial—of the true content of the options they faced. Knowledge of history and, I would say as a historian, the use of historical methods of research are essential for separating truth from legend, content from form, essentials from futilities, Holy Tradition from those human traditions that Jesus condemned before the Pharisees.

The idea of tradition is therefore inseparable from eschatology—the "conditional eschatology" revealed to us in scripture. It was inevitable that this eschatological dimension would be somewhat obscured with the establishment of Christianity in the Roman empire in the fourth century, and throughout the medieval and postmedieval periods. However, particularly in Eastern Orthodoxy, it never disappeared completely. It appears most clearly in the writings of the second century, as the second and third generations of Christians were coping with the problem of finding criteria of true doctrine in the face of the challenge of the competing gnostic traditions.

Tradition in the Second Century

Based upon the historical event of Christ's resurrection, the Christian faith depended entirely upon the eyewitnesses of Jesus. Indeed, Jesus Himself did not write anything, but only established a *community* of disciples, chosen by Him and entrusted with the ministry of being His witnesses. By the second century, all the members of that original community had died, and many were claiming to be their successors in the preservation of the authentic teachings of Jesus. Those whom we call the Gnostics included a variety of groups, carrying on a variety of traditions. One of their common claims was that they had secret, esoteric connections with Jesus through the mediation of covert teachings transmitted from one person to another and reserved for an elite of spiritual leaders ("Gnostics" means "people who have knowledge").

What means did Christians of the second century have to verify the teachings that were handed down in this way?

Although apostolic writings were in circulation, no New Testamental canon had yet been universally accepted: there was no formal basis for accepting the teachings contained in the Gospel of Matthew, or John, and rejecting those found in the gnostic Gospel of Thomas. The Church had no defined magisterium or central headquarters where authoritative decisions could be made in matters of doctrine or discipline. There was no way in which a Christian could say: "I believe this teaching because it is the Scriptures," or because "the magisterium of the Church has defined it." And, nevertheless, precisely during that period tradition not only proved itself to be an effective reality in the Christian Church, but also received its most convincing, most permanent—though sometimes paradoxical—definitions.

Two major Christian personalities played a particularly important role in this regard: St. Ignatius of Antioch (d.c. 107) and St. Irenaeus of Lyons (d.c. 202). It is not my intention to make a detailed presentation of their understanding of Christianity, but only to point at those aspects of their thought that have a permanent and, indeed, contemporary relevance for our understanding of Christian tradition.

For Ignatius, the structure of the Church is defined in terms of the Eucharist and, therefore, eschatology. Gathered for the Eucharist, the local community becomes the Catholic Church—not a part or a segment, but the plenitude. Indeed, "Where Jesus Christ is, there is the Catholic Church."[1] The constant appeals of Ignatius to his correspondents to be "obedient to the bishop" are based not on some external or formal power of the episcopate, received through some legal delegation, but upon the fact that the bishop presides at the Eucharist and manifests during the eucharistic meal the presence of Christ, or even of God the Father. Interestingly, Ignatius never mentions an "apostolic succession" of the bishops. The apostolic college is rather represented by the presbyterium, the group or college of elders who sit around the bishop during the eucharistic celebration as the apostles sat around Jesus at the Last Supper. Obviously, the Eucharist is seen by Ignatius in the same eschatological terms that

[1]*To the Smyrneans* 8.

appear in the book of Revelation, where the twenty-four elders ("presbyters") surround the throne during the angelic
singing of the *Sanctus* (Rev 4:4-11). The gathering of all
around the Eucharist, presided over by the bishop and the
presbyters, is, for Ignatius, the source of true teaching, as
opposed to that of all splinter groups. The truth appears as
a vision, as direct experience received in the local eucharistic
community, which expresses the "catholicity" or fullness of
the divine presence.

Almost a century later, Irenaeus envisages the Church on
a more universal scale—the threat of gnosticism was a common threat to all the local churches. He does not, however,
depart from the principles of the Ignatian perspective, maintaining the Ignatian idea of eucharistic catholicity in each
local community. Addressing himself to the Gnostics, he
writes: "Let them either change their opinion, or refrain from
making those oblations. . . . Our opinion is consistent with
the Eucharist, and the Eucharist supports our opinion."[2] But,
at the same time, he brings in the idea of "catholicity in
space":

> Having received this preaching and this faith, the
> Church, although scattered in the whole world, care-
> fully preserves it, as if living in one house. . . . Neither
> do the churches that have been established in Germany
> believe otherwise, or hand down any other tradition,
> nor those among the Iberians, nor those among the
> Celts, nor in Egypt, nor in Libya, nor those established
> in the middle parts of the world. . . . Neither will one
> of those who preside in the churches who is very power-
> ful in speech say anything different from these things,
> . . . nor will one who is weak in speech diminish the
> tradition.[3]

At the same time, Irenaeus bases his polemics with the
Gnostics on the idea of "catholicity in time," and this brings
in the notion of the apostolic succession of the bishops. He

[2]*Against Heresies* 4, 18, 5.
[3]*Against Heresies* 1, 10, 2.

uses this argument primarily to refute the gnostic claims of having preserved the true teachings of the apostles through secret, mysterious traditions, transmitted by word of mouth from one individual to another. The Church, on the contrary, according to Irenaeus, preserves tradition publicly, with bishops preaching it in the framework of their sacramental, eucharistic ministry within the community. Such is the meaning of apostolic succession: it is not a mechanical "validity" of ordination, but faithfulness in transmitting apostolic truth.

> The tradition of the apostles, made clear in all the world, can be clearly seen in every church by those who wish to behold the truth. We can enumerate those who were established by the apostles as bishops in the churches, and their successors down to our time, none of whom taught or thought of anything like these mad ideas [of the Gnostics].[4]

Irenaeus is very specific in affirming that the tradition is kept in *every* church. Indeed, his ecclesiology is the same as that of Ignatius: each local eucharistic community is "catholic" and possesses a fullness of grace and divine presence. But, in order to illustrate his point, he refers to the succession of bishops in "the very great, oldest and well-known" church of Rome, which possessed already in his time an "outstanding preeminence" in the West, where he was writing.[5] Immediately afterward, however, he also points to the apostolic succession in Smyrna and in Ephesus.

It is my conviction that the teaching of Ignatius and Irenaeus on tradition, with its sacramental and eschatological context, provides the essential basis for our own understanding of Christian tradition. Actually, the spiritual, intellectual, and social confusion that reigned in the late Roman empire is not without analogy in our own post-Christian world.

In later centuries, the concept of tradition was often reduced to legal categories of authority demanding obedience, and jelled into institutions inspired by political systems. The

[4] *Against Heresies* 3, 3, 1.
[5] *Against Heresies* 3, 3, 2.

episcopate itself progressively—but very early on—detached itself from its original meaning and function in the local eucharistic assembly and became a medieval administrative institution with jurisdiction over large geographic areas including many local eucharistic communities (or "parishes"). Emperors took the initiative in gathering "ecumenical councils," whose decrees were applied as state laws. In the West, to counter imperial power in the Church, the papacy itself assumed political power and gradually developed into the unique and obligatory criterion of true tradition. All these later developments overshadowed the original concept of tradition as it was understood and expressed by Ignatius and Irenaeus.

But is it possible today to transcend the historical past? Clearly not. Ignatius and Irenaeus cannot provide us with exact institutional models for the Church of today. However, without preserving or recovering the essential—eschatological and eucharistic—dimension of their understanding of the Church, a concept of Christian tradition today is impossible. Without such a recovery, it is impossible to distinguish Holy Tradition from purely historical, human, and therefore changing, forms of Christian life and belief. It is also impossible to transcend the opposition between conservatives and liberals, traditionalists and progressives, and to discover the sacramental continuity, throughout the centuries, of the communion of saints.

Of course, the theological question of whether a holy tradition exists at all, as distinct from human and humanly conditioned traditions, is a problem in itself, which is solved differently in the various confessional groups.

The Contemporary Ecumenical Situation

In raising the question "Does Christian tradition have a future?" one inevitably faces the fact of Christian disunity. If there is any issue upon which Protestants, Roman Catholics, and Orthodox have been historically divided, it is precisely tradition. Nevertheless, the present situation has been significantly modified not only by the ecumenical movement but also by drastic changes occurring within each of the three major families of Christians.

Contemporary Protestantism, in spite of its confessional and cultural pluralism, is united by its historic origin in the Reformation, which implied the rejection not only of the medieval Latin tradition in its doctrinal authority but also of the very idea of *any* authority other than Scripture. One of the major achievements of the contemporary ecumenical dialogue has been the recognition among many Protestants that no society can exist without tradition, and that the Reformed Christianity of the sixteenth and the following centuries is no exception. There is an increasing awareness of the role of tradition among Protestants, and there are, indeed, Protestant traditions, as expressed in "confessionalism" or "denominationalism." The principal of *sola scriptura,* the common acceptance of Scripture as the only ultimate criterion of Christian truth, did not and cannot produce ecclesial unity in history or doctrinal unanimity among the communities of the Reformation. Traditions still divide them today. This creates a very ambiguous situation, which appears particularly in the history of debates on this issue within the World Council of Churches. Indeed, within that body occurs a meeting not only among various Protestant groups, but also among such defenders of the idea of tradition as the "high church" Anglicans and, of course, the Orthodox.

On the one hand, many Protestant theologians begin to admit the utopian character of Christianity without tradition. On the other hand, partly because of their original prejudice in favor of the *sola scriptura* principle and partly because historical experience confronts them with the fact that the emphasis on tradition is, in practice, divisive, Protestants tend to identify tradition as a purely human—and therefore necessarily *relative*—element in Christianity. One inevitably holds some tradition, but one is justified in doing so only if one is fully tolerant of any other tradition as well. This acceptance of pluralism, often coupled with a definite relativism in doctrine, is particularly proper to American Liberal Protestantism: the various "denominations" are seen as being of purely historic origin and, as Reinhold Niebuhr has shown, reflect the social and ethnic history of American society.

Of course, within the Protestant community there is a unifying factor, the Bible, admitted by all. However, modern methods of biblical exegesis have uncovered its "human elements" as well, and therefore relativity, and therefore pluralism. Some modern ecumenists are even quite happy with an exegesis of the New Testament that makes sharp distinctions between a "Pauline," a "Johannine" or a "Lukan" Christianity, all equally legitimate, and whose discovery allows the legitimate coexistence of different Christian traditions as separate groups or churches. And, of course, if one defines a certain biblical doctrine as historically relative or socially determined, one can also easily challenge biblical authority for the solution of basic contemporary issues (for example, the role of women in the Church).

There is also a reaction against that liberal trend: fundamentalism, the blind and often naive acceptance of a literal inerrancy of the biblical texts, which implies refusal of history and of any form of cooperation between God and man in the act of revelation. The Bible is transformed into something it has never pretended to be: a universal, informational textbook about history and science.

What is lacking on both the liberal and the fundamentalist sides (which, of course, do not exhaust all of Protestant thought today) is the idea of communion between God and man in the sacramental and eschatological fellowship of the Church—a fellowship where catholicity or consistency in time is possible, where unity in space is desirable, and where the Bible should and can be properly and harmoniously understood both in its divine elements and in its human context.

In Roman Catholicism—as, of course, in Orthodoxy—tradition is a central reality in the existence of the Church. Furthermore, it stands at the very center of all the debates that have taken place since Vatican II. It has also been discussed for centuries between East and West. And these differences about the meaning of tradition actually led to the medieval schism between Rome and Orthodoxy. I have mentioned earlier that, already in the second century, tradition was recognized as the inevitable criterion of Christian identity vis-à-vis the Gnostics. Later, the innumerable debates on the Trinity, on christology, etc., that took place throughout the centuries could only be solved through reference to tradition. However, just as all parties involved referred to Scripture, so they also all invoked tradition. This was true of the Arians, the Nestorians, the Monophysites, the Iconoclasts and, indeed, of both the Greeks and the Latins when they clashed with each other over such issues as the Latin interpolation into the Creed (the *filioque*) or various other theological, disciplinary or liturgical issues. Generally speaking, the East insisted that all these problems be solved in their very substance through conciliar debates. They saw the apostolic tradition as entrusted to all the churches, which could therefore express it authoritatively only through consensus or conciliarity. This was not democracy, but rather a mystical belief in the full reality of Christ's and the Spirit's presence in each Eucharist, and therefore in the collective responsibility of the entire people of God for the preservation of the faith.

Humanly speaking, however, this was admittedly not a very realistic approach to the issues. It allowed controversies and debates to last for centuries, and emperors to interfere in Church affairs, seeking—generally without much success— to impose solutions by force. The Latin West gradually became realistic. Building upon the ancient respectability and prestige of the Church of Rome, it developed the idea that the bishop of that city—where the Church was founded by the apostles Peter and Paul—was the heir of Christ's promise to Peter: "you are Peter, and on this rock I will build My Church" (Mt 16:18). In that capacity, he was the final and ultimate criterion of true tradition, so that every conflict, every debate, every conciliar settlement ultimately depended upon a solution by him.

It is not my intention to engage here in a discussion of the origins and legitimacy of the Roman primacy, but only to point out its crucial importance for the understanding of tradition. First of all, I would point to the fact that—contrary to the antipapal polemics of all times—papal authority did not result from some ambitious, power-seeking plan of the pope to take over the leadership in the universal Church. If the Eastern belief in consensus of the churches was founded, as I said earlier, upon a mystical and eschatological perception of the Church, so was the belief in the special *charisma* of Rome. Indeed, it was not plainly described in Scripture, and not *clearly* sustained by early Church history. All informed Roman Catholic historians and theologians today recognize that the medieval papal authority was the result of a doctrinal and canonical *development,* which consisted in a gradual recognition by the Church of the fact that God had granted to His people a permanent leadership, able to regulate and to unify the local churches within a single, universal, disciplinary, and doctrinal structure.

Ultimately, the conflict between East and West resides in two conflicting spiritual perceptions of tradition. Is a solution possible today?

The "Constitutions" of Vatican II and the profound changes that have taken place within the Roman Catholic Church in the past two decades have all involved both the theory and the practice of tradition and, therefore, touched upon relations with the Orthodox Church. This process has been happening on different levels. Some effects were negative and divisive, while others present hopeful signs for the future. I will note three examples.

(a) The breakdown of monolithic discipline, which characterized the Roman Church in the past, has led to much confusion precisely because tradition had been identified too exclusively with authority: papal, episcopal, priestly. Traditions were now rejected because they were seen as imposed from outside. This led to new approaches to the liturgy, to the faith, to discipline. Seen with Orthodox eyes, some of these approaches were welcome—such as the use of the vernacular in the liturgy—while others were clearly divisive and negative—for example, secularization of the liturgy, suspicion of doctrinal consistency, etc.

(b) On the level of theological thought, post-Vatican II Roman Catholic theology, even if one excludes extreme cases like Küng's, is admitting much more widely than before the

historical relativity of doctrinal formulations. It tends to subject tradition to a radical hermeneutical reinterpretation,
similar to the critical exegesis introduced by nineteenth-century Protestant scholars in the study of the Bible. The decision
of an early Christian council or the statement of a pope is
seen as relevant (or only "probably relevant") in its own time,
but meaningless today. This approach, based upon modern
existential thought and linguistic analysis, allows for various
degrees of relativism in approaching tradition. And it raises
many problems. For instance, historical relativity in understanding the Old Testament scriptures is built into the very
nature of the material; indeed, for Christians, the value of
the Old Testament itself is *relative to* the coming of Christ,
which was being *prepared*. In the New Testament Church,
however, the *real presence* of Christ is a saving givenness,
a *liberation* not only from sin and death, but also from any
historical determinism. The relativization of truth is therefore
impossible; the living truth is manifested fully in Christ.
Although *words* and *expressions* used by ancient or medieval
councils are historically conditioned, their content and meaning are not. Tradition, therefore, is seen as *consistent* throughout the centuries. But where is this consistency to be found if
all doctrinal definitions are of relative value? Some would
perhaps say that unity in history is primarily to be found in
the *authority* that defines the truth, which can contradict itself
in order to meet different historical situations. But then there
is really no longer any hope of discovering a single Christian
Tradition. The problem of unity can only be solved by the
acceptance of a common authority—a direct return to the
absolutism of the medieval papacy—which would only be
called to admit greater pluralism within its jurisdiction.

(c) On the highest level of Roman Catholicism, that is,
the papal pronouncements themselves, there is also a new
search for a reinterpreation of tradition. I will mention only
one example, which is of great importance for the relations
between Rome and Orthodoxy. On the occasion of the seven
hundredth anniversary of the Second Council of Lyons
(1274), Pope Paul VI made a formal statement calling that
council a "council of the West" which mishandled the affairs

of the Eastern Church. Until that statement of Paul VI, the Council of Lyons was generally accepted in Roman Catholicism as an "ecumenical" council which sanctioned union with the East and approved the addition of the *filioque* to the Creed. Its categorization as only a "council of the West" would, of course, imply that it has no ecumenical authority. But if this is the case, other councils—for example, Florence or Trent or Vatican I or Vatican II—or formal doctrinal statements by popes that were never accepted by Eastern Orthodoxy are *also* reduced to the level of Western historical theologoumena, which Eastern Christians are under no obligation to accept.

Obviously, if this line of approach is pursued, the entire problem of the relationship between Rome and Orthodoxy appears in a new perspective. If Holy Tradition is defined not in terms of papal approvals—which were doubtlessly given to the Western pronouncements listed above—but in terms of reception by the entire Church, what exactly is the status of these pronouncements? And what about contemporary papal pronouncements? If these can all be ignored by Eastern Christians, can they also be formally criticized and denied? And if this right of criticism is given to Eastern Christians, is it not also obvious that Western Christians can criticize them too? Indeed, are the categories of East and West really applicable in our time, as they were in the Middle Ages? We are living in a small world, where cultures and traditions can no longer be seen in isolation from each other. Christian tradition must be present *as such*—in its universal existential significance—if it is to be accepted by our contemporaries.

What are the position and the contribution of the Orthodox Church in the inevitable debate on the nature of tradition? This position can be described both negatively and positively. In the negative sense, the Orthodox East has never been obsessed with a search for objective, clear, and formally definable criteria of truth, such as either the papel authority or the Reformed notion of *sola scriptura*. In a way that is often puzzling for Western Christians, the Orthodox, when asked positively about the sources of their faith, answer in terms of such concepts as the whole of Scripture, seen in the light of the tradition of the ancient councils, the Fathers, and the faith of the entire people of God, expressed particularly in the liturgy. This appears to outsiders as nebulous, perhaps romantic or mystical, and in any case inefficient and unrealistic. The Orthodox themselves defend their position as sacramental and eschatological. But are the other, supposedly clearly defined criteria more realistic and less mystical? Is not the belief in papal infallibilty also a mystical belief?

The practical result of the "nebulosity" with which tradition is defined in Orthodoxy is the deep sense that the entire Church—and not only the "authorities," whatever they may be, patriarchs or even councils—is responsible for tradition. Of course, an "ecumenical council" would be seen as the highest form of witness to the truth. But the Orthodox always point out that some councils of the past have been convened as "ecumenical" but were eventually rejected by the Church.

In practice, the absence of formal criterial or authorities, and the common responsibility placed upon all, leads historical Eastern Orthodoxy to a very conservative attitude. There is no ecclesial authority that would be able to *impose* changes or reform, not only as regards doctrine but even in liturgy or discipline. Changes, do take place, but they always require a slow process of "reception." In situations where the entire body of the Church lacks enlightened knowledge of the issues, both conservatism and changes are, of course, quite dangerous. Historically, Eastern Christianity has often fallen into a state of frozenness, where refusal to change is equated with traditionalism. On the other hand, as a reaction against conservatism, some rush into a race of progressivism, competing in this with Western Christians.

The most obvious and most significant challenges to Orthodox traditionalism today are, of course, the challenge of the socialist totalitarian society of Eastern Europe, where the largest numbers of Orthodox Christians live, and the opportunity offered by the relatively recent establishment of Orthodox churches in Western societies or in the Third World. Although quite different in nature, the forces which —in both of these situations—are challenging a Church that is so sacramentally oriented, so immutably doctrinal, so firm in referring to consistency with the past, are very strong indeed. The odds against the very survival of the Church in such circumstances seem overwhelming. Nevertheless, there are obvious signs of survival, progress, and renewal.

My paper has not given an answer to the question raised in its title: Does Christian tradition have a future? Perhaps no direct answer is possible. Actually, the New Testament itself gives no rosy picture of the success of the Christian message in history. It rather orients our minds and our hearts toward the eschaton, when, according to the promise, Christ will be all in all. This is why I began my paper by recalling the early Christian eschatological basis for the notion of tradition. Christian tradition cannot be reduced to the preservation of ideas and concepts, or to the definition of external, juridical structures serving to preserve the concepts. Both concepts and structures may be needed in history, but their role and significance are *relative*. They may and should change, but not their content, which is revealed in the mystery of Christ as new life, as liberation from both conceptualism and the law, and as an experience of the Unchangeable, who was incarnate of the Virgin Mary and became an indelible part of His own creation and of human history.

CHAPTER VI

Mission, Unity, Diaspora*

Until recently the word "mission" evoked primarily the activity of professional "missionaries" active in "non-Christian" countries with the help of their own mother-church. Before 1917, among the Orthodox Churches the Orthodox Church of Russia was practically alone in a position to support this classical missionary activity both within the political borders of imperial Russia and beyond (Japan, Korea, China, Alaska, etc.), and made a wide use of "missionary" methods. However, the word "mission" had a rather negative connotation among the Orthodox peoples of the Middle East, because it was used to designate Protestant proselytizing, unsuccessful among the Muslims but quite active among Eastern Christians.

Historical developments of the twentieth century led to drastic changes. Most Christians recognize that there are no more "Christian" countries whose duty it is to christianize "pagans" beyond the seas. They discovered that the "world" in need of Christ's gospel is at their very doors. The traditionally "Christian" countries in the West and in the East have been transformed into secular societies with Christian minorities.

Yet it appears that the Orthodox—at least in their accepted vocabularies and official attitudes—have not fully accepted the new situation. They still often speak and think in terms of

*Written on the occasion of the Thirtieth Anniversary of *Syndesmos.*

"Orthodox countries" and of an Orthodox "diaspora," implying a "normal" situation in the first case and a sort of transi-
tional, peripheral existence in the second. This situation is
harmful for two reasons. First, it shows an obvious lack of
historical realism. Neither the new secular societies established
in Eastern Europe, nor the Orthodox communities of the
Middle East, nor even Greece, can be seen today as Orthodox
Christian societies in the traditional and accepted sense of the
word. In practice the Church represents a minority in all these
areas, and in some of them this Orthodox minority has all
the sociological characteristics of a foreign "diapora," quite
detached from its immediate milieu. This does not mean, of
course, that all these ancient churches cannot envisage missionary possibilities for the future. To the contrary! Sometimes
their minority status has actually enhanced their spiritual
potential. This is certainly the case in some Churches in Eastern Europe. The ecumenical patriarchate of Constantinople,
deprived of its originally political basis, can recover (or acquire) a supra-national prestige, which will give greater
reality to its primatial *diakonia*. The patriarchate of Antioch
possesses a great potential for carrying on the ancient tradition of Arab Christianity within the Muslim majority. The
same can be true of the patriarchate of Alexandria, if it
consciously and totally assumes its missionary responsibilities
in Africa. But these potentialities will bear fruit only if the
Church, abandoning the myths of the past, recognizes itself
again as "the little flock," a "seed" thrown into a fertile
field, and identifies itself with its *mission* for the salvation
of humanity.

The second aspect which must lead the Orthodox to abandon the opposition between the purportedly "native" Orthodoxy and the "diaspora" is that this opposition represents a
grave *theological mistake*. The word "diaspora" refers to an
Old Testamental concept. In the Old Testament, God acted
in history through the mediation of a "chosen people," Israel,
to whom He had granted the "promised" land of Canaan,
where Solomon built a temple and where the Messiah was to
establish His reign. The Chosen People was called to cultivate
this land and possess it, and any exile from it was seen as

cursed by divine wrath. But the actual coming of the Messiah, born in Bethlehem and crucified outside Jerusalem's walls, revealed to humanity a new "promised land" in heaven, a new Jerusalem, expected to come all prepared (Rev 21:2), and showed the whole world to be a mission field. "Believe Me," said Jesus to the Samaritan woman, "the hour is coming when neither on this mountain nor in Jerusalem will you worship the Father. . . . God is spirit, and those who worship Him must worship in spirit and truth" (Jn 4:21, 24). Where is the "diaspora" then? The only acceptable answer to this question is that all Christians, whether they find themselves in Jerusalem or in the middle of the Pacific Ocean, are in diaspora, and that they reach the promised land only within the eschatological anticipation of the Eucharist and of prayer. Like the Jews of the diaspora, they are, anywhere in the world, "aliens and exiles" (1 Pet 2:11), having "no lasting city" and seeking "the city which is to come" (Heb 13:14), but also knowing that in Christ—*and only in Him*—they "are no longer strangers and sojourners, but . . . fellow citizens with the saints and . . . of the household of God" (Eph 2:19).

This is why the technical term "diaspora" is used in the New Testament only in the traditional Jewish, Old Testamental sense (Jn 7:35; Jas 1:1, 1 Pet 1:1), and it *never* appears in Orthodox canon law. Indeed, was it not St. Paul's major preoccupation to affirm that the new churches established by him in the midst of the pagan world were full-fledged *churches*, recognizing their spiritual ancestry from the mother-Church of Jerusalem, but in no way inferior to her in terms of the power of the Spirit and the presence of Christ wherever two or three are gathered in His name (Mt 18:20)? Orthodox canonical texts all aim at accommodating the fundamental structure of the Church to changing political and social circumstances, but never compromise the essential principle that the Church, as such, comes first. St. Paul, when the Corinthians wanted to split their community into several eucharistic assemblies, indignantly asked the question: "Is Christ divided?" (1 Cor 1:13). Similarly, the canons upheld the unity of the Church in every place; this was a way of maintaining Christians in their quality of "aliens and exiles," and of reminding them that their true "dispersion" (diaspora) is a separation from the Kingdom of God, not from some earthly, cultural home.

I fully understand, of course, that, very often, the word diaspora is used colloquially, and does not carry with it any conscious betrayal of the fundamental Christian vocation to be citizens of God's Kingdom. Furthermore, I do not want at all to minimize the spiritual riches and vigor of such authentic Orthodox "roots" as can be found in traditional Orthodox piety in Greece or in Russia, and which stand in so obvious contrast to the shallowness found in so many communities without either roots, or authentic missionary concern. I am only speaking of the unconscious spiritual mistake, so often made, of envisaging the present and the future of Orthodoxy as inseparably bound either to vestiges of a Byzantine political system, or to its illegitimate child, the secularized ethnic identification between nation and church, which occurred in the nineteenth century in Eastern Europe and the Balkans.

It seems obvious that if the contemporary Orthodox world is to recover an authentic missionary consciousness, it must overcome this spiritual mistake and recover that *catholicity of mind* which was so obvious in the apostles, the fathers, the saints, and which remains quite alive today in all *authentic* forms of the Orthodox tradition.

*   *   *

Our times witness a real revival of missionary spirit among many Orthodox. Participation in the ecumenical movement and a certain healthy emulation spurred by it have led to new ideas and concerns. But quite a substantial role in this revival was played by *Syndesmos*. Its original founders were already aware of the necessary connection between Orthodox unity— which was the main purpose of *Syndesmos*—and the Orthodox missionary responsibility. Indeed, it was at the Fourth General Assembly of *Syndesmos,* held in Thessalonika on September 4-7, 1958, that a formal decision was taken to create an "International Orthodox Missionary Society." A provisional Committee was appointed and a Secretariat was set up, headed by Anastasios Yannoulatos. The result of this decision was the establishment of the Center *Porevthentes* in Athens. Since that time, the Center and the various initiatives which followed have borne good fruits in East Africa and elsewhere.

However, the fundamental goal of *Syndesmos* was Orthodox unity; mission was seen as more than starting specialized missionary activities. Such activities were the necessary and creative expressions of a new spirit in serving the Church and in understanding Orthodox responsibility in the contemporary world. The remarkable vitality of *Syndesmos* in the following years; the constant support and blessings it received from the ecumenical patriarchate as well as from the other Orthodox Churches of which the various groups affiliated with *Snydesmos* were members; the geographical expansion of the membership, which today includes representatives from the entire Orthodox world; all place *Syndesmos* in a truly unique position for understanding what Orthodox mission to the world means.

As the resolutions of the New Valaamo Assembly (1979) show, *Syndesmos* has already become fully aware of the fact that one of the most obvious obstacles to the credibilty of the Orthodox witness today is the lack of canonical unity in areas where the Orthodox Church is most visible, where it is being observed and judged both by its friends and its critics alike, and, most importantly, by a secularized world in need of Christ's truth.

I have underlined earlier in this paper the basic ambiguity of the term diaspora, which is so often used to describe the situation of the Orthodox communities in countries like Australia, Western Europe, and America. My contention—based, I believe, on unquestionable biblical evidence—is that as long as these communities understand themselves as *diasporas,* they will be unable to fulfill their mission as *churches.* This does not imply at all, as many would think, that Orthodox immigrants in those countries must lose their original cultural identity and forget their ties with their motherland. Did not St. Paul boast of being of the seed of Abraham (2 Cor 11:22), a faithful Jew, willing to die for his people (Rom

9:3)? And still it is he who wrote and preached in Greek to the Greeks, and became the one, of all the apostles, to be the "apostle to the Gentiles." Through him indeed, the Spirit of God transformed the small group of Jesus' disciples into the Church Catholic.

But can one require everyone to be a new St. Paul? Is every Orthodox Christian up to such an apostolic consciousness? On an individual basis, of course not. But *the Church* herself necessarily accepts the model given by St. Paul as a practical example of her mission in the world. Otherwise, she simply cannot be the Church anymore! This is why true mission is always directed not only to those who are formally outside of the Church, but to insiders also. This mission can—and should—always imply some accommodation and flexibility, as Paul made himself servant to all, that he might win the more (1 Cor 9:19). The Church has always adopted the historical ways and ethos of the various nations. She adopted their languages and shaped their cultures. Quite legitimately she became Serbian in Serbia, and Georgian in Georgia . . . Similarly, in pluralistic societies like contemporary America, she can and must reflect the country's pluralism, and therefore serve the immigrants as well as the native Americans. However—and this is the crucial point—, she must be *in mission, serving* all people without becoming enslaved to anyone. St. Paul could become servant of all, only because he was "free from all men" (1 Cor 9:19). This freedom is precisely what is lacking when the Church identifies totally with ethnic diasporas, in fact renouncing the mission "to all." The problem is not that it helps the immigrants to preserve their human and religious identity, but rather that the Church accepts to be limited by the immigrants' particular interests and goals, which in turn are defined and supported by foreign ecclesiastical or political interests. The problem is not whether these interests are legitimate or not—they often are—but that they transform legitimate pluralism into *division.*

To make my thought quite clear on this point, I would like to stress that difference between the necessarily pluralistic mission of the One Church in a pluralistic society, and the disaster of a divided Church which loses its capacity to accomplish its mission. There is nothing harmful in an Orthodox ministry to Russian emigrés in France, or to Greek-speaking Americans in America; but the mission of the Church is obscured when native Frenchmen or Irish Americans are called to become Russians or Greeks when they join the Orthodox Church, and when the Church itself, officially and vociferously, defines itself as "Russian" or "Greek."

It is at this point that my original objection to the term diaspora is, I hope, clarified. The problem is not whether *de facto* ethnic diasporas exist or not—they obviously do, although they lack the theological and spiritual dimensions of the Jewish diaspora—but the problem is whether *the Church as such* is able to stand above them, to unify them, to exercise her pastoral ministry for them, leading them to the Kingdom of God—in other words, whether she exercises her mission as One, Holy, Catholic and Apostolic.

As is well known, the issue appears on the agenda of a forthcoming Holy and Great Council. However, open discussion of the subject is continually delayed. The positions of the various autocephalous Churches have been made public. These positions do not always coincide with each other, but Orthodoxy does not recognize any other way to solve disagreements than the way of conciliarity. On the other hand, it would be quite naive to think that a Holy and Great Council —when and if it meets—will be able to solve the issue without preliminary debate and serious preparation. It is my strong belief that *Syndesmos* can and should actively contribute to this debate. Actually, it began doing so at the Valaamo Assembly.

Personally, if I were in a position to make a formal proposal to the forthcoming Council, I would move that the following text be adopted, implying a special responsibility of the ecumenical patriarchate for its implementation:

"In areas and countries where two or more Orthodox autocephalous Churches are sending clergy to exercise a permanent ministry, canonical order requires the establishment of a united Church. Procedures to be followed are to be elaborated by consultation between all parties involved on the universal or local level. Pluralism of language and traditions will be maintained and guaranteed wherever necessary, through the establishment of appropriate structures organized on a temporary basis."[1]

Such a text—or a similar one, corresponding to the nature of the Church—would insure that the Orthodox Church will really assume and pursue its mission in countries where its existence is mistakenly seen today as one of a foreign-oriented diaspora.

[1]This proposal was originally published in *The Greek Orthodox Theological Review* 17 (1972) 1:41-50; reprinted in my book, *Living Tradition* (Crestwood, NY: St. Vladimir's Seminary Press, 1978) pp. 99-107.

CHAPTER VII

One Bishop in One City*

No canonical regulation has ever been affirmed by the Tradition in the Church with more firmness than the rule which forbids the existence of separate ecclesiastical structures in a single place. The strictly territorial character of Church organization seemed practically self-evident to the Fathers of all the councils, and it is implied by all the canons dealing with ecclesiastical order. We shall here try to give a brief analysis of this canonical legislation of the Church and a definition of its theological and spiritual meaning.

The Canons

The Orthodox Church has not, as yet, provided her faithful with a complete system of canonical legislation. It is even doubtful whether she will ever do so. The fullness of divine truth and life indeed abides in the Church, and no juridicial system will ever be completely adequate to this living and organic reality which true Christians know only by experience. What, then, is the real meaning of our canons? As soon as we are acquainted with their text, we discover that they usually have been issued in relation to specific situations and distortions of ecclesiastical life which occurred in the past. In order to understand them fully, it is necessary to be

*Previously published in J. Meyendorff, *Orthodoxy and Catholicity*, New York, 1966, pp. 107-118.

acquainted with the particular historical circumstances in which they were published. Then it is that the eternal and normative value of the canons becomes manifest. They appear as a kind of medicine applied by councils and Church Fathers to cure specific diseases of the ecclesiastical organism. This cure is a product of the eternal and permanent nature of the Church. It was, and still is, a witness of the unchangeable identity of the Church, its inner organization and structure being established upon the apostolic witness and provided with the constant presence of the Holy Spirit. The canons indicate to us how to apply to the changeable realities of human history this unchangeable and vivifying reality of the redemptive grace of God abiding in the Church. Consciously to disregard the canons of the Church leads finally to corruption of Church life, that is, to ecclesiological heresy.

In order to understand correctly each canon of the Church, we must, therefore, first localize it in its proper historical setting, then define the particular aspect of the eternal nature of the Church to which it corresponds. Regarding the question which now occupies us—the territorial structure of the Church in the Orthodox tradition—no serious question of interpretation arises, and both the formulas and their meaning are absolutely clear.

Several ecumenical councils have issued decisions on the matter, and the historical situation in which these decisions were made was not really different from ours today. These decisions from the highest authority in the Church are obviously expressions of Holy Tradition, so that we may safely affirm that, by their very consistency, they express the true and permanent nature of the Church.

The First Ecumenical Council, called in 325 in Nicaea by Emperor Constantine, dealt mainly with the doctrinal question of the Arian heresy. It had also to pay attention to the remnants of various struggles which had divided Christians in the time of the persecutions. Among these dissensions was the schism of the Novatians, a sect of puritans that refused forgiveness to those Christians who had betrayed the faith during the persecutions; second marriages also were formally condemned by this sect. After peace was given to the Church by Constantine, many Novatians wished to return to the communion of the Church. Canon 8 of Nicaea defines the mode through which Novatian communities were to be reunited. Since no question arose as to the validity of Novatian ordinations, the episcopal dignity was to be granted to their bishops, but only in places where no parallel orthodox hierarchy already existed. "But wherever there is a bishop of the Catholic Church," proclaims the Council, "it is obvious that, as the bishops of the Church will keep the dignity of a bishop, the one called a bishop among the so-called puritans shall have the honor of a presbyter. . . . There may not be two bishops in the city."[1] It would obviously have been easier to solve this Novatian problem by giving the schismatic bishops some honorary title, or else by transferring them to some empty episcopal see, or by keeping them as heads of their churches, thus establishing two parallel, mutually recognized "jurisdictions" in the same place. But the Council decided otherwise and solemnly proclaimed the principle of territorial unity of the Church.

In a somewhat different historical context, the Second Ecumenical Council (Constantinople, 381) formulated the same principle on the level of provincial ecclesiastical administration. Because the Church of Alexandria at that time had shown the tendency to intervene and perform ordinations in provinces which did not belong to its jurisdiction, especially in Constantinople, the Council ordered in Canon 2 that, "The bishops are not to go beyond their own diocese to churches lying outside of their bounds, nor bring confusion on the churches . . . And let not bishops go beyond their dioceses for ordinations or any other ecclesiastical ministrations, unless they be invited. And the aforesaid canon concerning dioceses

---

[1]The major canonical texts of the Orthodox Church are readily available in English. The canons of the Ecumenical Councils are published by H. R. Percival, *The Seven Ecumenical Councils of the Undivided Church: Their Canons and Dogmatic Decrees,* in *A Select Library of Nicene and Post-Nicene Fathers,* 2nd series, Vol. XIV (Grand Rapids, MI: Eerdmans Pub., 1979). Cf. also the sometimes confusing translation of the standard canonical collection of the Greek-speaking Churches, the "Pedalion" or "Rudder" compiled in the late eighteenth century by St. Nicodemos of the Holy Mountain, which has been published in the United States by the Orthodox Christian Educational Society (Chicago, IL: 1957).

being observed, it is evident that the synod of every province will administer the affairs of that particular province as was decreed in Nicaea." The Third Ecumenical Council also declared, in relation to the Church of Cyprus: "None of the God-beloved bishops shall assume control of any province which has not heretofore, from the very beginning, been under his own hand or that of his predecessors" (Canon 8). Finally, we find the same principle in Canon 20 of the Quinisext (Sixth Ecumenical) Council: "It shall not be lawful for a bishop to teach publicly in any city which does not belong to him. If any shall have been observed doing this, let him cease from his episcopate."

A single bishop in every local community, a single synod or council in every province—such is the absolute rule established by the Fathers. In the course of centuries the Church had to protect this rule against many attempts to alter it by the establishment of different principles of ecclesiastical administration. The importance and the authority of some churches led them to exercise a power over an area larger than their own ecclesiastical district and to "bring confusion on the churches." We already saw the Second Ecumenical Council dealing with Alexandrian pretentions of this kind. Gathered in Carthage in 419, the bishops of northern Africa, traditionally opposed to the interventions of Rome in their provincial affairs, wrote to Pope Celestine that "all matters should be terminated in the places where they arise" and that the Fathers "did not think that the grace of the Holy Spirit would be wanting to any province." No bishop, patriarch, or pope can put himself above the council of bishops of a given province "unless it be imagined that God can inspire a single individual with justice, and refuse it to an innumerable multitude of bishops assembled in council."[2] The ecclesiastical affairs of a province cannot be solved from far off, "from behind the see," as the African bishops put it, since the only true aim of Christians is to promote and establish the Kingdom of God in every place, not to serve the interests or ambitions of any particular church or individual.

The same territorial principle was applied in 692 by the

[2]Percival, ibid., p. 510.

Council *in Trullo* (Sixth Ecumenical, or Quinisext) to a case very similar to our contemporary situation: the Cypriot immigration into Asia Minor. Wars between the Arabs and Byzantines provoked shifts of population in the border regions, and one of these shifts concerned, in 691, the larger part of the population of Cyprus which was transferred by Emperor Justinian II to the district of the Hellespont, near the sea of Marmara.

Ecclesiastically, the district possessed in Cyzicus its own metropolitan whose election was confirmed by the patriarch of Constantinople. Strictly speaking, the Cypriot bishops, who followed their flock into exile, should have submitted to this local jurisdiction. However the archbishop of Cyprus (since the time of the Council of Ephesus, 431) was the head of an autocephalous Church. The General Council of 692 decided to preserve his former right in his new jurisdictional area. The only way of doing so, without encroaching on the territorial unity of the Church, was to submit the metropolitan of Cyzicus to the former archbishop and also to delegate to him the primatial rights of Constantinople over the area of Hellespont. Both actions were taken by the Council (Canon 39): "We decree . . . that new Justinianopolis[3] shall have the rights of Constantinople and whoever is constituted the pious and most religious bishop thereof shall take precedence of all the bishops of the province of the Hellespoint and be elected by his own bishops according to ancient custom . . . the existing bishop of the city of Cyzicus being subject to the metropolitan of the aforesaid Justinianopolis . . ."[4]

It is quite obvious, therefore, that the autocephalous status of the Church of Cyprus did not give her any right to establish her own ecclesiastical administration in places which already possessed a local ecclesiastical structure. The Council

[3]Justinianopolis was then the name of Constantia, the capital of Cyprus. The Cypriot settlement in Hellespont was called "New Justinianopolis."

[4]Percival, p. 383; see also the commentary on this canon by Bishop Nikodim Milash, *Pravila Pravoslavnoi Tserkvi s tolkovaniiami,* Vol. 1. (St. Petersburg, 1911) pp. 524-525; and by St. Nicodemos of the Holy Mountain in the "Rudder," p. 335. The Cypriots later returned to their home island, but their archbishop still keeps among his honorific titles that of "Bishop of New Justinianopolis" or "New Justiniana."

did not admit the creation of a parallel Cypriot jurisdiction in Hellespont, and so preserved territorial unity. It solved quite radically a question of precedence at the expense of the existing authorities—Constantinople and Cyzicus—but it did not divide the Church. The pattern of ecclesiastical structure remained the same: one Church, one bishop, one community in every single place. The canons of the Church have always protected this simple principle against all attempts to create several separated ecclesiastical administrations in the same place or country, and also against the tendency of some big and important Churches (Rome, Alexandria, Antioch) to deprive the local bishops of their authority and to affirm their own power over the rights of the local synods.

The Nature of the Church

The aim of the Incarnation of the Son of God and the very purpose of His teaching, death, and resurrection was to establish between God and men a new relation, a new unity: "The glory which Thou hast given Me I have given to them, that they may be one even as we are one, I in them and Thou in Me, that they may become perfectly one, so that the world may know that Thou hast sent Me" (Jn 17:22-23). Unity with God supposes also unity among men, a unity which is described here by Christ Himself as visible to the world and as a witness concerning His own mission. It is by seeing the unity that Christians have among themselves that the world "knows" and "believes." This unity is not, therefore, only a spiritual and invisible reality, but it appears in the concrete, visible life of the Church. Without Christ's unity, Christians cannot truly fulfill their call, because the world cannot see in them the new life given in Christ.

This is the reason why, at the very origin of the Church, "all who believed were together and had all things in common" (Acts 2:44). Christians gathered together regularly for the celebration of the Lord's Supper and nothing—not even the Roman persecutions—could prevent them from holding their assemblies, because the very nature of their faith implied that God abided not in each of them individually, but in the entire Church, the Body of Christ. Only by being a member of this Body could the individual also be a member of Christ. Early Christians considered each church assembly, held in the name of Christ, that is, in unity and love, as witness of Christ's victory over human egoism, selfishness, and sin. A first-century Father, St. Ignatius, Bishop of Antioch, wrote in a letter to the Church of Ephesus: "Be zealous to assemble more frequently to render thanks [*eucharistein:* "to celebrate the Eucharist"] and praise to God. For when you meet together frequently, the powers of Satan are destroyed and danger from him is dissolved in the harmony of your faith."[5]

No other passage of early Christian literature gives a clearer indication of the very mystery of the Christian Church: by the power of the Holy Spirit, scattered and separated human beings are able to become, when they gather, a powerful and victorious transfigured reality: "Where two or three are gathered in My name, there am I in the midst of them" (Mt 18:20). This real presence of God in the assembly of the Church makes it possible for the various Christian ministries to be really Christ's mysteries, and this applies, first of all, to the episcopal function. Every Christian community is manifesting the Body of Christ in its fullness since this Body cannot be divided: "Where Jesus Christ is, there is the Catholic Church."[6] The function of the bishop is to fulfill in the assembly the ministry of the Head, to sit where Christ sat among His disciples, to teach what He taught, to be the shepherd and the high priest. "Let all follow the bishop," St. Ignatius writes, "as Jesus Christ did the Father, and the priests, as you would the apostles . . . Let that Eucharist be held valid which is offered by the bishop or by one to whom the bishop has committed this charge. Wherever the bishop appears, there let the people be."[7] There is no Church without

---

[5]*Ephesians* 6, 13; translated by G. G. Walsh, *The Fathers of the Church, The Apostolic Fathers* (New York: 1947) p. 92.

[6]Ignatius of Antioch, *Letter to the Smyrneans* 8; *ibid.,* p. 121. This is the earliest example of the adjective "catholic" applied to the Church in Christian literature.

[7]*Letter to the Smyrneans;* ibid. In the time of St. Ignatius, every Christian

the bishop, but the reverse is also true, there is no bishop outside of the Church, since the head needs a body to fulfill its function. In the views of St. Ignatius, which are confirmed by the entire Tradition of the Church, it is in the Eucharist that the divinely instituted episcopal ministry finds its real meaning. However, the Eucharist is the sacrament of our unity with God and of our unity in Christ among ourselves. The bishop stands at the very center of this mystery. His sacramental functions in the eucharistic liturgy are also expressed in his pastoral responsibilities which oblige him to assure, in the practical life of the Church, the unity given sacramentally by God in the Eucharist. His ministry is, therefore, one of reconciliation and unity.

All these aspects of Orthodox ecclesiology constitute the foundation of our canonical legislation concerning Church structure.

It is inadmissible to have two communities and two bishops in a single place, simply because Christ is one, and only one person can fill His place. This point is of a particular importance today in our dialogues with Roman Catholics who have begun to realize that the existence of one "vicar of Christ" for all the churches duplicates (if it does not suppress) the episcopal sacramental ministry of each particular local community. In Roman Catholicism, there can be less theological or practical objections to maintaining in a single place several ecclesiastical jurisdictions, separated by rite, language, or nationality, because the criterion of their unity and the center of their ecclesiastical life is always to be found in Rome, outside their own limits. On the contrary, Orthodox ecclesiology, in affirming the catholic fullness of every local Church, is bound to manifest catholic unity everywhere on the local level. The presence of Christ in the Church is guaranteed by the very "gathering in His name," in the unity of the true

community (or "parish") was headed by a bishop who normally was the only celebrant of the Eucharist. Later, with the expansion of Christianity, the bishops started to delegate their privileges to priests on a permanent basis. The parish priest is nowadays the normal center of Church life on the parish level, but he cannot fulfill these functions unless he is appointed by the bishop.

faith, and in conformity with true tradition—and not by an allegiance to some universal center.

What happens, then, when Orthodox Christians living side by side in the same city consider it normal to constitute several "churches"—the Russian, Greek, Serbian, or Syrian—which, of course, maintain their formal unity in faith and spirit, but not in practice? There is no doubt that such a situation is the greatest blow to our witness in the contemporary world and goes against the very nature of the Church of Christ. Any reference to "spiritual unity" or "sacramental intercommunion" is of no relevance in this connection because Christ has established on earth a Church visibly one and because the meaning of spiritual communion consists precisely in giving us the strength and responsibility to accomplish visible unity.

Conclusion

The Tradition of the Church being clear on this point, both on the canonical and on the doctrinal level, the only question which may arise is whether strict territorial unity—one Orthodox bishop and one Orthodox Church in every place for all nationalities and groups—is practical and practicable today. I would answer this question in a twofold manner.

First, by historical evidence. Until the early twenties of the present century, when the united Orthodox Church of America (in the Russian jurisdiction) began to disintegrate into an entire constellation of parallel national jurisdictions, it was impossible to find in the entire history of the Church any example of the territorial principle being overlooked. Do we have the right, then, to consider our present situation as normal?

Second: Orthodox canon law admits what is called the principle of "economy." The most competent canonists of our time are unanimous in defining this principle as a conscious relaxation by the ecclesiastical authorities of the letter of the canons in cases when a strict legalistic observance would do more harm than good to the entire body of the Church.[8] Let us, therefore, act slowly and carefully "for the good of the Church." For a relatively long period of time, we must give the greatest attention to the existence in America of various national groups preserving their national identity. This can easily be secured inside a united Church. National organizations and societies will have to be maintained for the next few generations, and it is equally unavoidable that parishes, deaneries, and even dioceses will preserve for some time their national character. However, a single Church structure must unite and coordinate Church life in America. Various concrete needs can be covered by the principle of "ecclesiastical economy," but division cannot remain a permanent norm, and, at the same time, it is to be remembered that the "good of the Church" which may justify temporal separation requires also unity. The final and ultimate challenge to all of us begins when this "good of the Church" *conflicts* with the interests of our respective national groups. There is no doubt that, in this case, any Orthodox Christian, be he bishop, priest or layman, is bound to put the will of God and the Holy Tradition of the Church above the "human traditions" which were condemned by the Lord as soon as they conflicted with the law of grace. With wisdom and care, let us move toward the restoration of Orthodox canonical norms in America.

[8]H.S. Alivizatos, *Economy from the Orthodox Point of View* (in Greek) (Athens: 1949) pp. 31-39; Jerome Kotsonis, *Problems of Ecclesiastical Economy* (in Greek) (Athens: 1957) pp. 30 ff.

CHAPTER VIII

The Council of 381 and the Primacy of Constantinople*

"The bishop of Constantinople must receive privileges of honor (τὰ πρεσβεῖα τῆς τιμῆς) after the bishop of Rome, because that city is a New Rome" (Council of Constantinople, 381, canon 3). This is the first time that the Church of Constantinople appears in any canonical text. The earlier Council of Nicaea and the councils of the fourth century never mentioned it. The obvious historical reason for this novelty is that, at the end of the fourth century, Constantinople became, more explicitly than before, the new capital of the Empire.

1. Historical context

In 381, we are historically at the end of the long Arian crisis. Arianism is vanishing from the scene. In the western, Latin-speaking part of the Empire, the Emperor Gratian has restored Orthodoxy in 378. Gratian is a good friend of Ambrose, Bishop of Milan since 374. Both are Nicaean-Orthodox, and one could say that the West is now firmly

*A lecture delivered at the Orthodox Center of the Ecumenical Patriarchate Chambésy, Switzerland, in May, 1981, and published also in *Les Etudes Théologiques de Chambésy. 2. La Signification et l'actualité du IIe Concile oecuménique pour le monde chrétien d'aujourd'hui*. Chambésy, 1982, pp. 399-413.

behind the faith of St. Athanasius. In view of its own particular theological approach to the Trinity, emphasizing the
unity of God, rather than the personal characteristics, it had
always fewer problems with the ὁμοούσιος of Nicaea than
the East.

By 380, the Emperor Theodosius I the Great has become
sole emperor. Upon his crowning as emperor in 374 in
Thessalonika, he received baptism. Therefore, Theodosius is
really the first Christian Roman ruler, because the emperors
preceding him were baptized only upon their deathbed. They
were not quite sure how to be both a Christian and an emperor at the same time, and therefore were postponing the
problem until the end of their lives. But Theodosius was
baptized at his coronation, apparently in connection with a
sickness, where he was in danger of losing his life. As a
baptized Christian, he participated in the liturgy of the
Church. Upon his entry in Constantinople, he projected a new,
Christian image of the Empire, and his Christianity was
Nicaean-Orthodox.

However, there was no absolute unity among the Orthodox, but a polarization between those whom historians usually
name the "old-Nicaeans," and the so-called "neo-Nicaeans."
The old-Nicaeans stood for the letter of the statement adopted
by the council of 325. St. Athanasius had been fighting for
this statement, which affirmed the consubstantiality—the
ὁμοούσιος—of the Son with the Father, without any further
qualifications. His argument had been primarily soteriological:
the Son of God, Jesus Christ, the Logos, is God consubstantial
with the Father because He is the Savior. No one else than
God Himself can save man.

This formula of Nicaea—ὁμοούσιος—was not quite
acceptable to many theologians of the East, especially those
who were the disciples of Origen. For them, the word
ὁμοούσιος was associated with Modalism, which had been
formally condemned by the Council of Antioch in 268. Furthermore, the word was seen by most Easterners as a *philosophical term* associated with Modalism (i.e. three persons
in God seen only as "modes" of One God). Even when they
had no Arian sympathies, they were reluctant to accept it.

It is only the great unifying work performed by the Cappadocian fathers, St. Basil the Great and the two Gregories, which secured the peace of the Church in the East. The Cappadocians were fighting for the ὁμοούσιος, but were also affirming the existence in God of the three *hypostases*. Their acceptance of Nicaea was therefore a qualified one, hence the term "neo-Nicaean" which designates them.

The neo-Nicaeans accepted the Nicaean faith, together with the doctrine of the three hypostases. They recognized the danger of Modalism. Instead of a formal, "fundamentalist," acceptance of Orthodoxy, they further explained the faith; they met the legitimate questions, the legitimate doubts of some people, and expressed the faith in a living way.

The theological disputes between the old-Nicaeans and neo-Nicaeans led also to personal as well as institutional conflicts, especially in the churches of Constantinople and Antioch. Who were the old-Nicaeans in 381? First of all, the western part of the Church was necessarily "old-Nicaean." It never understood very well the doctrine of the three hypostases, expressed in Greek by the Cappadocians. There was a long-standing language problem between East and West on this point. Also, the Church of Alexandria seemed to stand for the letter of Nicaea. Peter of Alexandria, successor of Athanasius, did not want to add anything to what Athanasius had already said. Finally, in Antioch, a small group also firmly stood behind the old-Nicaean formula. The group was led by a bishop named Paulinus, who had been consecrated by a very interesting Latin bishop named Lucifer of Cagliari who, during the Arian controversies, had been traveling around the East, ordaining old-Nicaean bishops. But the largest group, the "great church" at Antioch, was neo-Nicaean. It was headed by Meletius, a friend of the Cappadocian fathers and a reasonable man, who accepted the Nicaean faith together with the doctrine of the three hypostases. Paulinus considered him non-Orthodox. In addition to the "Super-Orthodox" party of the old-Nicaeans, headed by Paulinus, Arianism was alive too, in Antioch.

Major problems arose in Constantinople also. Before the restoration of Orthodoxy, St. Gregory of Nazianzus—"the

Theologian"—had been called to the capital to head the little group of Orthodox Christians in a private home. He used the house-church—called the Ἀνάστασις—to preach Orthodoxy. It is there that Gregory delivered his famous theological orations which were seen as the classical expression of Cappadocian theology. But now that Theodosius had assumed power in Constantinople, Gregory was chosen—against his own will, and against all expectation—to become the bishop of Constantinople with full imperial support. He was, of course, the great spokesman for the neo-Nicaean faith, but faced strong opposition on the part of the Church of Alexandria, which stood on old-Nicaean positions and, at the same time, was very unhappy with the rise of Constantinople as the real center of Eastern Christianity. Thus, Alexandrian bishops consecrated their own candidate as bishop of the capital, a competitor to Gregory of Nazianzus, called Maximus the Cynic. This Maximus, in spite of his name which sounds a little pejorative, was apparently an Orthodox and quite respectable person, with whom Gregory of Nazianzus himself had corresponded. Apparently, he was called the Cynic because he had long hair which made him look like the philosophers called the κυνικοί—the Cynics. But this was a reference to his external appearance, not to his convictions or behavior. Theodosius put some order to things: he expelled Maximus and installed Gregory of Nazianzus. Maximus the Cynic went to the West, where he was well received, since the old-Nicaean position was also that of the Church of Rome, whereas neo-Nicaean Orthodoxy established itself in Constantinople.

The council which Theodosius called in May 381 to settle the affairs of the Church was only later recognized as the Second Ecumenical Council. It was composed exclusively of Eastern bishops, and Theodosius took for granted that the neo-Nicaean position expounded by the Cappadocian Fathers was an adequate expression of Orthodoxy. He did not want the faith debated anymore. In fact, it appears that doctrine was not even on the agenda of the Council. There was an edict by Emperor Theodosius published on February 28, 380 already, and another one on January 10, 381, which proclaimed the Nicaean faith, with the understanding that the Cappadocian Fathers were its most authoritative exponents. No minutes of the Council survived. The only dogmatic or theological debate which might have taken place, was possibly connected with the appearance at the council of the "Pneumatomachoi" —thirty-six bishops who denied the divinity of the Holy Spirit. But they did not stay for long, since their theological position was obviously not acceptable to the Fathers. Gregory of Nazianzus, as bishop of Constantinople, had already delivered his sermons on the Holy Spirit, affirming the Spirit's divinity. He even chided St. Basil, because St. Basil practiced some οἰκονομία in not calling the Holy Spirit "God," in order not to antagonize the moderate "Pneumatomachoi." No such *oikonomia* was extended to them in 381. The Council was comprised of approximately 150 bishops, all from the East (except Egypt), and the major problems on the agenda were the schisms of Constantinople and Antioch. In principle, the question of Constantinople was settled in advance by Theodosius, and the Council probably just accepted the imperial decision. Gregory of Nazianzus was officially welcomed and aclaimed a bishop by Meletius of Antioch. The latter, who headed the neo-Nicaean "Great Church" in the Syrian capital, was chairman of the Council. But Alexandrian opposition was also giving a strong moral boost to the "old-Nicaean" party of Paulinus. Gregory, using his prestige with the emperor, tried to accommodate the two Orthodox parties in Antioch. He proposed that they should make peace with each other; if Meletius died first, Paulinus would be accepted as bishop. But this peaceful proposal of Gregory of Nazianzus was rejected, and his letters contain some bitter reflections on the debate. The vast majority of Eastern bishops supported Meletius, and thought it absolutely improper to capitulate before Paulinus, who had been ordained by a Western intruder, Lucifer of Cagliari. The old-Nicaean party appeared to them not only as an "Alexandrian," but also as a "Western" party.

A kind of eastern patriotism stood behind Meletius: "Christ rose in the East," cried the bishops. But Gregory of Nazianzus, the peacemaker, answered that Christ was also crucified in the East. He did not succeed in pacifying the

Antiochian factions, and Meletius was finally recognized as the only bishop.

In the midst of these debates, representatives of the West also arrived at the Council. They were headed by Acholius, Bishop of Thessalonica. Indeed, the Balkan peninsula, and its major city, Thessalonica, were part of the Western empire and therefore belonged to the jurisdiction of the Roman pope. At his arrival, Acholius was accompanied by Timothy of Alexandria, and both of these powerful church leaders gave their support to the cause of Maximus the Cynic and Paulinus of Antioch. The situation was further worsened by the unexpected death of Meletius, who was replaced by Gregory of Nazianzus who, as local bishop, became also chairman of the Council. But his personal position was weak. His enemies were looking for reasons to challenge his authority. They remembered that, before his coming to Constantinople, he had been bishop in Arianzum. Early church practice did not allow transfers of bishops from one diocese to another, and many saw his election as uncanonical. The good Gregory of Nazianzus, who was not made at all for ecclesiastical politics but for theology and for writing poetry, decided to quit, after having occupied the throne of Constantinople for less than a year: he officially resigned his position and retired to a country estate. Theodosius then gave full support to the Eastern bishops. Acholius and Timothy left the capital. Nectarius, an old senator who was not even yet baptized, was elected bishop of Constantinople. Baptized and consecrated in a matter of days, he symbolized the victory of the Eastern neo-Nicaean party over Alexandria and Rome.

Such was the Council, whose 1600th anniversary we celebrated in 1981. Its major theological avhievement is in the fact that it restored Nicaean Orthodoxy in the East, as formulated in the theology of the Cappadocian Fathers. But this triumph happened in the midst of serious problems—personal, political, and ecclesiastical—which are reflected in the canons issued by what was later recognized as the Second Ecumenical Council of Constantinople. Of the seven canons found in the collections, only the first four are considered by historians as being authentic. The last three were published in 382 by another council, held also in Constantinople. Therefore, there is no difficulty in affirming that canon three, which sets Constantinople as having the πρεσβεῖα τιμῆς, "privileges of honor" after Rome, is indeed an authentic canon of the Council of 381.

Before I go into the analysis of the canon itself and its background, let us recall the aftermath of the Council. The Council ended, but the old-Nicaean party was not reconciled. In the West, two Councils met in 382, one in Aquileia and the other in Rome, which gave support to Maximus and Paulinus. Therefore, the Council of 381 was held out of communion with the Church of Rome. Pope Damasus supported the old-Nicaean minority. Furthermore, neither St. Basil the Great (who died in 379), nor Gregory of Nazianzus were actually in communion with the Church of Rome. They never thought that this placed them outside of the Church. Eventually, the Church of Rome would accept the Council of 381, but apparently not before the sixth century.

2. Canonical meaning

In the light of all these events, it is easier to understand the significance of canon 3, which grants the bishop of Constantinople πρεσβεῖα τιμῆς, "privileges of honor." Certain churches had enjoyed πρεσβεῖα since the beginning of the fourth century, as described in the first part of canon 6 of Nicaea: "Let the ancient customs (ἀρχαῖα ἔθη) be preserved in Egypt, Libya, and Pentapolis, so that the bishop of Alexandria may have power over all those areas, because the same custom exists with the bishop of Rome." In other words, canon six affirms the existence of a regional primacy of the bishop of Alexandria in North Africa, and justifies it by the same practice which exists in Rome. This famous and very significant text, establishing a parallel between Alexandria and Rome, describes *regional* primacies. It does not settle the problem of the later Roman claims. Indeed, historians spent much ink and paper to find out which primacy of Rome is implied in the text. It was certainly *not* the universal primacy, since the Council does not speak of a universal primacy of Alexandria: rather it affirms that Alexandria has a regional primacy, because the bishop of Rome also has a regional primacy.

The second part of canon 6 reads: "Also in Antioch and in other provinces (ἐπαρχίαι) the honorary privileges (πρεσβεῖα) must be preserved for the churches."

Now this second part of the text provides the general sense of the term πρεσβεῖα, which are recognized as belonging to three churches: Rome, Alexandria, and Antioch. In fact, more precisely, the canon grants πρεσβεῖα to Alexandria, by reference to models already existing in Rome and Antioch. Indeed, at Nicaea, the bishop of Alexandria was *de facto* a leading figure, and had his own interest and prestige sanctioned in this canonical text. This was a moral, traditional authority, which did not, however, possess any juridical implications. But, as sanctioned by the Council of Nicaea, it was acquiring some canonical substance. The bishop of Alexandria became a sort of patriarch for Egypt.

The same notion of πρεσβεῖα reappears in canon three of Constantinople; the πρεσβεῖα are now given to the bishop of the imperial capital.

Before we go further into our understanding of canon three, let us also read canon two of the same Council of Constantinople. It speaks of some prominent bishops of the Church who, just like those bishops who are invested with πρεσβεῖα, are exercising an authority over and above that of the local bishops. They are called οἱ ὑπὲρ διοίκησιν ἐπίσκοποι: "the bishops over a diocese." For the understanding of the text it is essential to go back to the Greek original, which is not always properly rendered in the various translations, which often confuse terms like διοίκησις and ἐπαρχία. These are civil, not ecclesiastical terms, designating administrative divisions of the empire. An ἐπαρχία is a "province" which is not very big—like a Swiss canton in size—several cities, but not too many. A διοίκησις, is, however, a large section like Asia, the Pontus, and Thrace. There were three διοικήσεις in Asia Minor, each one having twenty or so provinces. So, what appears in canon two is a new category:

an ἐπίσκοπος ὑπὲρ διοίκησιν: a bishop exercising authority over an entire diocese. The Council of Nicaea (325) had established a system according to which the bishop of the "provincial" capital (μητρόπολις) presided over the local synod of bishops with the title of "metropolitan" (μητρο-πολίτης). But in the canons of Constantinople, there are "bishops over dioceses." There is no clear definition of what they do and what their rights are, because the canon only says what they should *not* be doing. The ὑπὲρ διοίκησιν ἐπίσκοποι, who are also later called ἔξαρχοι, should not go to churches beyond their "diocese" (ταῖς ὑπερορίαις ἐκκλησίαις) and should not mix their churches together but, according to canon 2, the bishop of Alexandria should care for the affairs of Egypt only, the "bishops of the East" (that means the diocese of the East, with Antioch as its capital) should administer only the affairs of the East (while preserving the privileges—πρεσβεία—of the church of Antioch), and the bishops of the diocese of Asia should care only for Asia. The same is true for Pontus, Thrace, and so on. The canon goes on to say that the bishops should not perform consecrations beyond the borders of their diocese. The historical circumstances which we have described earlier explain why canon 2 was published in 381: Bishop Peter of Alexandria had just consecrated Maximus the Cynic as bishop of Constantinople! The text is entirely oriented against Alexandria, and also against Lucifer of Cagliari, i.e. the bishops from the West or from Alexandria who were interfering in the affairs of the church of Constantinople—a church beyond the borders of their dioceses. In order to understand the significance of this canon fully, we should turn our attention to the Byzantine commentaries published in the twelfth century during the Comnenian period, by Aristenos, Balsamon, and Zonaras. These commentaries entered the authoritative tradition of Orthodox canon law. Balsamon in particular gives an interpretation of the canon which is important for understanding the primacy of Constantinople. He begins his commentary by reminding the reader that the sixth and the seventh canons of the First Council have already established which dioceses should be submitted to the pope of Rome and to the bishops of Alexandria, Antioch, and Jerusalem. Canon 2 of the Second Council provides a regulation about the dioceses of Asia, Pontus and Thrace, which were not mentioned in 325, and which, therefore, do not belong to the jurisdiction of any one of the four original "primates." Paraphrasing the canon, Balsamon recalls its stipulations that bishops should limit their activities to their own provinces. He continues by recalling the changing character of church organization in Asia Minor and elsewhere, and describes the development of patriarchal centralization. At the same time, he acknowledges existing exceptions. Here is his well-known text:

"Note that, according to the text of the present canon, all the provincial metropolitans were, in the past, autocephalous, and were ordained by their own synods. But this system was changed by the 28th canon of Chalcedon, which specified that the metropolitans of the dioceses of Pontus, Asia, and Thrace, as well as certain others indicated in the same canon, should be ordained by the patriarch of Constantinople, and be submitted to him. But do not be astonished if you find other autocephalous churches, such as the church of Bulgaria, the church of Cyprus and the church of Iberia (Georgia). Indeed, Emperor Justinian honored (in this way) the archbishop of Bulgaria . . ., whereas the Third (ecumenical) Council honored the archbishop of Cyprus . . ., and a decision of the synod of Antioch honored (the primate) of Iberia. For it is reported that in the days of the Lord Peter, patriarch of the Great Antioch, the City of God, there was a synodal disposition making the church of Iberia, which was then submitted to the patriarch of Antioch, free and autocephalous" (Ράλλη-Ποτλῆ, Σύνταγμα Κανόνων, II, pp. 171-172).

This text shows that Balsamon understands canons 2 and 3 as part of a single development leading toward greater centralization of the ecclesiastical structures around major centers: Rome, Alexandria, Antioch, and now Constantinople. The twelfth-century commentator also understands that the older decentralized system, when all provincial primates or "metropolitans" were "autocephalous," can be maintained in particular cases. The three examples of Bulgaria (i.e. Ohrid), Cyprus, and Georgia provide him with the opportunity of defining three ways by which, in his opinion, the status of autocephaly can be recognized: an imperial decision in the case of Bulgaria, a decree of an ecumenical council in the case of Cyprus, and a disposition of the mother-church (i.e. Antioch) in the case of Georgia. No other Orthodox canonical text defines the procedures leading to autocephaly in a way clearer than this one, and autocephaly itself is understood as the preservation of an ancient order, when a council, or the emperor, or the mother-church considers it proper.

The new process of centralization, well described by Balsamon, was indeed the main canonical result of the Council of 381. This process, however, did not only express itself by preventing Alexandria from meddling in the affairs of the dioceses of Asia Minor, but it established the primacy of the "New Rome." Three churches so far enjoyed "honorary privileges": Alexandria, Rome, and Antioch; now there is also Constantinople. But in the latter case, the "privileges" are exceptional: Constantinople receives not only πρεσβεῖα τιμῆς, but πρεσβεῖα τιμῆς μετὰ τὸν τῆς Ρώμης ἐπίσκοπον; in other words, it is second after Rome, because it is the New Rome, and ranks above Alexandria. The motivation here is clearly political. There is actually no other reason for Constantinople to have these πρεσβεῖα except that it is the New Rome. Much later, in the Middle Ages, when the polemics with the Latins would start, the church of Constantinople used the tradition of St. Andrew's preaching in Byzantium in order to prove that it is also an "apostolic" church. But neither Emperor Theodosius nor the Council of 381 seem concerned with "apostolicity." They know only the obvious facts of Rome as the old capital of the Empire, and of a "New Rome" in Constantinople. Apostolic foundation, on the other hand, is a common thing in the East: Antioch, Corinth, Thessalonica, and many other churches were founded by apostles, but never claimed primacy based on this fact. Alexandria also claimed to have been founded by St. Mark, but this was certainly not the decisive reason which explains its dominance in the East: indeed, St. Mark is not even one of the twelve apostles. It is clear, therefore, that if "apostolicity" was not a decisive factor in determining the regional primacies of

such ancient sees as Alexandria and Antioch, it did not play
any real role in the case of Constantinople either. Political
and social realism alone explain the granting of πρεσβεῖα
τιμῆς to the bishop of the "New Rome" in 381.

The connection affirmed by canon 3 between the "privileges of honor" granted to the bishop of Constantinople, and
the fact that that city was the "New Rome" implied that the
"privileges" had no geographical limits: "Rome" was always
synonymous with universality. The bishop of the capital was
not, therefore, simply a "bishop over a diocese" (ὑπὲρ
διοίκησιν ἐπίσκοπος) as his colleagues of Alexandria or
Antioch, endowed with regional primacies. However, the
nature of his—implicitly universal—"privileges" was not
further defined. One would have to wait until the Council of
Chalcedon (451) to find such a definition. And there was
another point on which the brief text of canon 3 lacked
clarity: the relationship between the *two* Romes. The realistic
or political logic which motivated the canon seemed to require
that the "New" Rome—which was the actual capital of the
Empire—receive primacy over the "Old." Nevertheless, the
canon specifies that its privileges placed the bishop of Constantinople "after" his Roman colleague.

Some Byzantines attempted to solve the difficulty. Thus,
Anna Comnena, daughter of Emperor Alexis I and author of
a history of her father—the famous *Alexiad*—writing in the
late twelfth century, gives a purely chronological significance
to the preposition *after*. Attacking the universalist idea of the
papacy promoted by Pope Gregory VII (1073-1085), she
proclaims that Old Rome has been replaced by the New, both
in civil and ecclesiastical matters: "When the empire was
transferred from Rome to our country, to our imperial city,
so was also the Senate, and the entire government, and the
order of the priestly thrones. The emperors of old granted
privileges to the throne of Constantinople. And, in particular,
the council of Chalcedon gave to the bishop of Constantinople
the first place and submitted to him all the dioceses of the
world" (I, 13, 4). However, a few decades later, John
Zonaras formally contradicts Anna's interpretation: "Some
people," he writes "understood the preposition 'after' as

implying not inferior honor, but the chronologically posterior establishment (of Constantinople)." He refutes this view, and maintains that the preposition "after" shows inferiority and lesser position (ὑποβιβασμὸν καὶ ἐλάττωσιν)," (Ράλλη-Ποτλῆ, Σύνταγμα Κανόνων, II, pp. 173-174). Balsamon also affirms that the Old Rome enjoys a hierarchi-cally—and not only chronologically—superior honor (ibid., p. 175).

Aware of the consciousness which the bishop of the Old Rome possessed of his own position in the universal Church, and rejecting it, the Byzantine commentators of the twelfth century were nevertheless reluctant to follow the "realistic" logic of Anna Comnena to its conclusions. They were leaving a door open to a dialogue on the nature of the Roman primacy—a dialogue, which is possible only if one envisages the canons in their ecclesiological significance and dimensions.

3. Ecclesiological significance

The Council of 381 defined the moral primacy of Con-stantinople without giving it any geographical limits; a parallel was established between the moral primacy of Old Rome and the πρεσβεῖα τιμῆς of the New Rome. It gave no clear juridical or canonical definition of the rights and the powers of Constantinople, but only the affirmation of its primacy of honor. In 451, however, the Council of Chalcedon gave to this moral primacy some legal and canonical content. In canon 28, it refered to canon 3 and expanded it in terms of concrete rights and duties.

The process through which Constantinople was first recog-nized as having some moral "privileges," and then saw its privileges interpreted in terms of formal "rights," was fol-lowed in all known cases of "privileged" churches. We have noted earlier how canon 6 of Nicaea invoked "ancient cus-toms" to justify the "privileges" of Rome, Alexandria, and Antioch. These were later transformed into patriarchal "rights." Since "ancient customs" could not have existed in the case of

Constantinople, its moral "privileges" were granted to its bishop in 381, and defined jurisdictionally in 451.

In order to interpret this process, there is no other recourse than Orthodox ecclesiology, which, on the one hand, recognizes the absolute, ontological identity of all local Churches with each other and, on the other hand, requires that they live and act in unity. The "primacies" of some Churches are defined—first morally, then jurisdictionally—as tools for securing unity of the churches: such definitions can only be made through ecclesial consensus (i.e. conciliarity) and, obviously, cannot create "super-bishops" invested with power over the other churches: primates are responsible before the churches in their ministry of unity.

In the contemporary Orthodox theology of the Church, there is a remarkable agreement in focusing ecclesiological models upon the image of the Eucharist—the Mystery in which each local church becomes really and fully the Catholic Church. This agreement is witnessed in the work of Nicholas Afanassieff, of John Zizioulas, and also in the *History of the Ecumenical Patriarchate,* by Metropolitan Maximos of Sardis. The "eucharistic" ecclesiology described by these authors, who may disagree on some individual aspects of the issue, but not in the central intuition, is the one described in the writings of St. Ignatius of Antioch, and which finds itself in continuity with the New Testament itself. A local church is a concrete local community gathered around the Eucharist and presided by the bishop. St. Ignatius expressed a reality which for him was obvious, as coming out of the original event which happened at Pentecost, when the Holy Spirit descended upon the apostles gathered in Jerusalem. There was no revolution in the first century or at the end of the first century in favor of an Ignatian theory of a *monarchical episcopate,* as some historians have sometimes supposed, because such a revolution would have met with resistance. The Ignatian letters were accepted as normative without debate, which could have happened only because they reflected the inner consciousness of the Church. Ignatius writes: "Where Jesus Christ is, there is the Catholic Church" (*Smyrn.* 8), which means that the Catholic Church is the fullness of the presence of Christ and the Holy Spirit in the Eucharist; that the number of faithful is irrelevant, the important thing being that they are gathered in the local community around the bishop in the Eucharist. Indeed, the Pauline image of the Church as the Body of Christ is also fully applicable here. The Body of Christ cannot be divided, but it is present fully whenever the Eucharist is celebrated. Christ cannot be submitted to secular categories, such as numbers, universalism, or power. Christ alone renders the Catholic Church catholic. The one who presides at the Eucharist is necessarily pronouncing the words which Christ has pronounced, he is really the image of Christ. There cannot be any "power" over him, except Christ's. I believe this ecclesiology to be *the basis,* the nucleus of Orthodox ecclesiology itself. However, eucharistic ecclesiology has some dangers, if misunderstood; the major danger being a congregationalist interpretation, the affirmation of a kind of self-sufficiency of each local church. Indeed, while each local church has the fullness of the presence of Christ, this fullness exists on the condition that it is in union with all the other churches. No local church can be "catholic" in isolation. This is what Cyprian of Carthage, the great bishop of the Church in the third century in North Africa, understood particularly well: "The episcopate is one," he wrote, "and therefore each bishop holds the fullness of his episcopate *in solidum.*" He has it all, provided he has it together with others. The Church can be Catholic and the ἐπίσκοπος can exercise his episcopate only within the unity between the Churches. So, just as unity in the Eucharist or in the local church is essential for catholicity, so too, is unity between the local Churches. The one is inseparable from the other. Orthodox canon law—all the canons—can be understood precisely as expressing or protecting this unity locally, or this unity between the local Churches. Thus, canons require the participation of all the bishops of a province in the ordination of a new bishop, after his nomination by the clergy and laity of his own local church. The legislation of the Council of Nicaea (325) goes in the direction of having Church organization match the political structure of the Empire; each "province" (ἐπαρχία) has its own episcopal synod. Thus, the unity of the episcopate is secured primarily for consecrating other bishops, and fits the convenient pattern of an existing administrative setting.

If the local bishop expresses local sacramental unity, if the metropolitan (the bishop of the major city of each province) presiding over the synod, expresses this unity of the episcopate on the provincial level, so higher primates gradually assume the coordination of the episcopate on a wider scale. This was the case of bishops called "exarchs of dioceses," and later "patriarchs." However, since the unity of the Church—and, therefore, the unity of the episcopate—must also manifest itself on the universal level, there were certain "privileges of honor" always attributed to a "first bishop" of the world episcopate. This was the case of James, in Jerusalem, as he appears in Acts 15. Later the bishop of Rome assumed the "privileges" in virtue of an unchallenged consensus of all the local Churches.

However, these "privileges" did not—and could not—imply in themselves any special sacramental power (which fully belonged to each bishop in his local Church), or any power of jurisdiction over other Churches. No such jurisdiction—for example in the case of provincial metropolitans presiding over the consecration of bishops—existed without a formal conciliar decision. Councils indeed began to define the jurisdictional power of the "first bishop," but never went beyond granting Rome the right of summoning ecclesiastical courts of appeal when it received appropriate petitions from parties dissatisfied with the judgment of their own provincial synods (Council of Sardica). Similar rights were also granted to Constantinople (Chalcedon, canons 9 and 17). Otherwise, the position of the first bishop remained one of moral authority and of spiritual leadership—the only kind of "privilege" which was consistent with early Christian ecclesiology. A formal conciliar decision could, of course, have given it a more concrete and precisely-defined legal content, but this did not happen, except in the form of a right of appeal. Basically, the "privileges" remained of a moral nature.

In the case of Rome, immense authority was exercised by some popes (e.g. Leo I, or Gregory I), but, in other instances

—for example during the Arian controversies of the fourth century, or the period of decadence, suffered by the papacy during the tenth—the leadership of Rome was practically absent. In the case of Constantinople, which became the "first see" of Orthodoxy after the schism, there were similar variations in the existential reality of leadership: personalities, as well as political circumstances, gave it more or less content at different epochs. However, the Orthodox Church never either denied the existence of a "first see," or proceeded with defining more clearly than had been done in Sardica (343), Constantinople (381), or Chalcedon (451) the canonical rights of its incumbent.

In the Middle Ages, there are numerous instances when the patriarch of Constantinople acted, in fact, as the real head of the entire Church of the East. For example, the "Great Council" of St. Sophia (879-880) describes Pope John VIII and Patriarch Photius as two equals, united in faith and responsible before each other in disciplinary matters (canon 1). Similarly, in the last period of the Byzantine Empire, as the imperial government was reduced to begging and exercised little power beyond the city of Constantinople itself, the patriarchate was able to preserve and even to reinforce its authority and influence throughout the Orthodox world. It happened then that some patriarchs defined their role in terms similar to those adopted by medieval popes, even if some allowance should be made for rhetorical exaggeration. Thus, Patriarch Philotheos, addressing Russian princes in 1370, would call himself "the common father, established by the most high God, of all the Christians found everywhere on earth" (Miklosich-Müller, ed., *Acta Patriarchatus Constantinopolitani,* I, p. 516). "Since God," he writes in another letter, "has appointed Our Humility as leader (προστάτην) of all Christians found anywhere in the inhabited earth, as solicitor and guardian of their soul, all of them depend on me (πάντες εἰς ἐμὲ ἀνάκεινται)" (ibid., p. 521). The patriarch continues by defining the role of bishops, appointed to sees in any part of the world, as being his personal representatives.

This somewhat extreme interpretation of the "privileges"

of Constantinople was not completely abandoned after the fall
of the city (1453), when the ecumenical patriarch became the
head of the Christian *millet* within the Ottoman Empire.
However, beyond the Ottoman borders—particularly in Russia
—his influence and prestige was low. This does not mean that
the Russians ever seriously upheld the theory of "Moscow the
Third Rome," for it is from Constantinople that they sought
and obtained the recognition of their patriarchate (1589-
1593), and it is still Constantinople which provided them
guidance in the liturgical reforms of the seventeenth century
which caused the disastrous and anti-Greek schism of the "Old
Believers."

At no point was there in Orthodoxy a denial of the fact
that a certain ministry of unity belongs to a "first bishop."
But this ministry was always understood in moral terms,
rather than in terms of formal power, or rights. The actual
exercise of this ministry depended upon political circumstances, as well as the orthodoxy, the wisdom, and the prestige
of the "first bishop" himself. This was the case during the
first millenium of Christian history when "Old Rome" enjoyed primacy, as well as in the second, when, in virtue of
canon 3 of Constantinople (and canon 28 of Chalcedon), this
primacy belongs to Constantinople. Both centers lived through
dark periods. Both made mistakes which lowered their prestige, but it is only when the "Old Rome" decisively and
consistently pretended to transform its moral "privilege" into
actual jurisdictional and doctrinal power that the Orthodox
East refused to follow it.

4. *Contemporary problems*

Disunity on the world scale is one of the most obvious
weaknesses of the Orthodox Church today, and therefore the
nature and practice of leadership by Constantinople, as a
center of unity, is a crucial element in all pan-Orthodox
endeavours.

Following the model which was shown on the very day
of Pentecost, when representatives of many peoples heard

the apostles preach in their own tongues, the Orthodox East has always accepted the principle that each nation has the right to worship God in its own language. The West followed a different pattern, enforcing Latin, but it also—frankly and decisively—adopted the Eastern practice at the Council of Vatican II. But the use of a language is not a purely formal matter; it involves mental attitudes, aesthetic feelings, and even theology. The use of many languages by the Church is a decisive option, which allows for cultural pluralism, but also implies unity. The apostles to the Slavs, SS. Cyril and Methodius, understood this very well, and took the option very deliberately. They defended the Slavic liturgy because it allowed newly-baptized Slavs to understand the Word of God. They also praised the very idea of a cultural variety, but in the One Catholic Church. Indeed the miracle of Pentecost, as shown by the Byzantine Orthodox hymnology, sanctifies variety but not disunity. The distribution of tongues "calls all to unity" because the One Spirit transcends the sinful divisiveness which triumphed at the tower of Babel, when the tongues were "confused." Thus, variety is an enriching sign of catholicity, whereas division is sin.

Unfortunately, after centuries of missionary expansion and cultural pluralism, which did not then prevent Orthodox unity, the Orthodox Church today suffers from divisiveness. The model of Pentecost implies that the One Catholic Church becomes the common home of all nations without prejudice to their cultural identity. Of course, if this were not the case in Orthodoxy today, it would not be the Church anymore. But the divisive forces of secularized culture and secularized nationalisms, adopted from the Western Enlightenment and dominating the national revivals of the nineteenth century, have imperceptibly changed attitudes and mentalities. Instead of the Church making a legitimate use of cultural pluralism in order to make its message heard and better understood, the various nationalisms are making use of the Church in order to achieve their own goals. There is still unity and plurality, but there has also been a subtle but radical reversal of spiritual priorities. The various national Churches, which used to lead the national and cultural revivals in their respective countries, are being reduced to the role of modest and antiquated tools, used by secular, and often anti-Christian, forces for the pursuit of goals totally foreign to the gospel as such. The Church, which won the respect and admiration of pagan Rome, which created the Christian civilization of the Byzantine Commonwealth and of so many Orthodox nations, which has survived centuries of Islamic domination and is now surviving despite the Communist Revolution, is accepting to be domesticated, as an element of ethnic national consciousness, instead of transforming all provincialisms into factors of wider catholicity. The issue is one of evangelic mission. The apostles were sent by Jesus "to teach all nations": this does not mean that nations are to be suppressed or lose their identity, or that the universal Church is to become a uniformed stereotype, but it does mean that its servants cannot serve any higher interest than that of the Christian faith in its catholicity.

We have already insisted on the point that Orthodox Catholicity has always been based on the preservation of a certain pluralism and polycentrism. It is therefore normal that today the Orthodox Church is a family of local Churches, and that most of them are national Churches, deeply rooted in the history and the culture of their peoples. Within their own respective countries this gives them additional prestige and strength. But how is the Orthodox Church to present a unified witness on the world scale? Certainly, by showing its unity in faith. But if our unity in faith is real, what about a united action, a united mission, a united *diakonia* in the world, which knows no barriers and which aspires after an Orthodoxy which is not only Greek or Russian, but can also become African, American, or Asian?

In this respect, our national, ethnic, or cultural commitments, while not evil in themselves, constitute real cover for *de facto* separatism. They inhibit the missionary spirit, and hide the universal nature of the Church. This is particularly evident in areas, which are—misleadingly—called "diaspora." Indeed, the very concept of diaspora belongs to the Old Testament times, when true religion had a God-established "home" in the land of Canaan. In the New Testament, the New Jeru-

salem is made present wherever the Holy Eucharist is celebrated, so that Christians can be at home everywhere, while
remaining "strangers" in any place of the world.

The canons of the Councils also clearly require that the
common "home" in the Eucharist, wherever it is found, be
reflected in the unity of the episcopate and of Church structure. The permanent existence of separate "churches" in the
same place is a mockery of our Orthodoxy Christian commitment. It is fortunate that, at the end of the last century, on
the eve of the emergence in historical Orthodoxy of the major
problems faced by us today, the Council of Constantinople
(1872) clearly condemned "the heresy of phyletism," which
consists in "the establishment of particular churches, accepting
members of the same nationality and refusing members of
other nationalists, being administered by pastors of the same
nationality," and as "a coexistence of nationally defined
churches of the same faith, but independent from each other,
on the same territory (Quoted in Maximos of Sardis, Τὸ
Οἰκουμενικὸν Πατριαρχεῖον ἐν τῇ Ὀρθοδόξῳ Ἐκ-
κλησίᾳ, Thessalonike, 1972, pp. 323-25).

This text speaks for itself. There is no time to discuss
here the historical circumstances under which it was issued:
formally, it condemned the Bulgarians, who were attempting
to establish a separate church organization on the territory
of the ecumenical patriarchate. But the Bulgarians were certainly not alone guilty of "phyletism"! It is clear therefore
that the text of 1872 should apply to all, and all should accept
the judgment of the council which issued it.

But, many would ask, is the requirement *practical?* Is it
realistic to demand a forceful and artificial merger into one
"supranational" Church of individuals and communities, at
the expense of their cultural habits and emotional attach-
ments? The answer to this question can only be given on two
different levels. Indeed, on the level of the faith, the gospel
of Jesus Christ is neither "practical," nor "realistic." Shall
we then betray it? But, on the other hand, provided one
recognizes the *norm,* and therefore the ultimate *goal,* and
provided one follows other principles of the gospel, such as
charity and understanding of the "weak," one will also find

the "practical" and "realistic" way to assure unity in plurality, in mutual respect and mutual enrichment.

It is at this point that "privileges of honor" of the first bishop could—and should—manifest themselves in wise leadership. Obviously, the normal canonical order cannot be achieved except through conciliarity: the ecumenical patriarchate can and should channel and direct it. There is no way in which it can *impose* solutions, because it possesses no formal right to do so, but it can help local churches to solve their problems and new local churches to emerge. Its powers are strictly moral, but it can successfully exercise them if it remains itself above phyletism and above the pursuit of particular interests, including its own. Its present weakness could actually enhance its moral strength, if it becomes obvious to all that it is not the instrument of some external power, but is looking only for the interests and unity of the Church; if it sincerely tries to inform itself about the real issues; if it uses a competent and international personnel in managing its ministry of leadership.

Personally, I see no way in which the Orthodox Church can fulfill its mission in the world today without the ministry of a "first bishop," defined not anymore in terms which were applicable under the Byzantine Empire or in terms of universal jurisdiction according to the Roman model, but still based upon that "privilege of honor" of which the Second Ecumenical Council spoke. We should all think and search how to redefine that "privilege" in a way which would be practical and efficient today. I believe that the tradition of the Church offers sure guidelines in this respect.

Is the patriarchate ready to welcome this common search? Are we ready to abandon provincialism, defensiveness, and nationalistic arrogance, in order to be faithful—as our fathers in the faith have been—to the tradition which the early Councils and the Fathers have entrusted to us? Let this be, before additional damage is brought to our credibility, to our own sense of integrity, and to the mission of the Orthodox Church in the contemporary world.

CHAPTER IX

Russian Bishops and Church Reform in 1905*

In principle and in law, the reforms of Peter the Great attempted to integrate the religious functions of Russian society with the centralized imperial administration. Thus, Russian Orthodoxy was considered not really as a "church," enjoying a degree of autonomy, but merely as a body of beliefs shared by the emperor's subjects and requiring state-sponsored social and educational services. Its new organizational structure was designated as the Department of Orthodox Confession (*Vedomstvo pravoslavnogo ispovedaniia*).

Obviously, Peter's system did not adequately express the traditional Orthodox conception of the Church. Even the Byzantine medieval pattern, enshrined in the Orthodox canonical collections, presupposed a "symphonic" relationship between the empire and the priesthood, not the absorption of the latter by the state.[1] Whatever might be said of the Byzantine pattern's practical application in Muscovite Russia (where the power of the tsar was in fact more arbitrary than that of

*A lecture delivered during a Conference on Russian Orthodoxy under the Old Regime at the University of Minnesota, Minneapolis, Minn., in April 1976, and published in R. L. Nichols and Th. G. Stavrou, *Russian Orthodoxy under the Old Regime,* University of Minnesota Press, Minneapolis, 1978, pp. 170-182.

[1]Cf. F. Dvornik, *Early Christian and Byzantine Political Philosophy. Origins and Background,* Dumbarton Oaks Studies, no. 9 (Washington, D.C.,

the Byzantine basileus), this idea of "symphony" implies a theological distinction between the ultimate functions of Church and state: only distinct realities can function "symphonically"; a department is simply a cog in the state machinery.

Many serious historical studies assume that the Russian clergy lived largely in ignorance of the system's inadequacies, and instead, clergymen supposedly enjoyed a privileged position and opposed any reform of the status quo. The superficiality of this stereotyped notion can easily be demonstrated by examining the statements of bishops in a most significant publication, the three volumes of their official *Replies* (*Otzyvy*) to an inquiry addressed to them on July 27, 1905. The Holy Synod had asked the Orthodox hierarchy to describe those features of Russian Church life which in its view needed reform or alteration.[2] Despite the brief time allowed for preparing their answers (by December 1905), the bishops replied punctually. Their comments thus represent a spontaneous, sometimes improvised, reaction to a sudden opportunity for free discussion. The overprocurator had expected the bishops to hold conservative views: one does not normally expect from them revolutionary—or even reformist—thought, Nevertheless, with near unanimity the Russian prelates favored reforms and, even more importantly, they achieved a significant theological and ideological consensus about the principles for greater independence which they considered desirable for the Church.

This consensus indicates that independent thought—an important condition for spiritual freedom—had remained alive even within the rigid framework constructed for Russian Orthodoxy by Peter and his successors. Moreover, the *Replies* disclose the educational and intellectual background of their authors, their spiritual genealogy in the preceding decades and even centuries, and their remarkable willingness to

1966) I-II; also my article "Justinian, the Empire and the Church," *Dumbarton Oaks Papers*, XXII (1968) pp. 45-60; repr. in John Meyendorff, *The Byzantine Legacy in the Orthodox Church*, St. Vladimir's Seminary Press, Crestwood, NY, 1982, pp. 43-66; also more briefly is the author's

[2]*Otzyvy eparkhial'nykh arkhiereev po voprosam o tserkovnoi reforme*, 3 vols. (St. Petersburg: 1906) and *Pribavleniia*.

recognize and grapple with the theological and canonical issues of the day, including the problems of the lower clergy and laity. Nearly unanimously they demanded the convocation of a church council, proposed innovations for both provincial and central church administration, and foresaw for the clergy a greater role in the country's social and political life.

Farsighted and educated churchmen, including lay professors in the ecclesiastical academies, had always regarded Peter's reformed church as abnormal and canonically unjustifiable. Many shared the distaste of the Petrine system expressed by the authoritative Metropolitan Filaret (Drozdov, 1782-1867) of Moscow. The *Replies* show that generally by the beginning of the twentieth century, the Orthodox hierarchy shared the optimistically reformist mood of the intelligentsia. Churchmen widely accepted A.S. Khomiakov's idea of *sobornost'* as the necessary framework for any possible schemes of reform. These attitudes help explain the several formal steps taken toward church reform in 1904-5. Hence the impetus did not result from any spectacular revolutionary upheaval, but rather from a convergence of opinion among bishops, the intelligentsia, and the leading elements of the clergy. Divergent opinions, of course, soon appeared, but the original reform impulse contained the remarkably uniform view of all these groups.[3]

Under pressure from public opinion, particularly from the *zemstvo* congress held in November 1904, the government enacted a decree on religious toleration abolishing many of the restrictions for non-Orthodox religions. The newly permitted toleration of other churches sharply emphasized how severely the state ruled and controlled the "privileged" official religion, and the indignation provoked by this realization led to the publication of three important statements. As it turned out, these statements proved to be the first steps

[3]For a general review of the events see A. Bogolepov, *Church Reforms in Russia, 1905-1918* (Bridgeport, CT: 1966: reprinted from *St. Vladimir's Seminary Quarterly,* 1965); cf. also J.S. Curtiss, *Church and State in Russia: The Last Years of the Empire, 1900-1917* (New York: 1940, reprinted 1965); James Cunningham, *A Vanquished Hope: the Movement for Church Renewal in Russia, 1905-1906,* Crestwood, NY: St. Vladimir's Seminary Press, 1981.

leading to the council of 1917-18. Political obstacles, however, created delay.

Metropolitan Antonii (Vadkovskii) of St. Petersburg produced the first statment in the form of a memorandum (*zapiska*) to the tsar and the Committee of Ministers, requesting "a special conference of representative of the Church's hierarchy, with the participation of competent persons from the clergy and the laity." No government official was to be included. The conference would devise proposals providing the Church with autonomy and the "right of initiative," guarantees of "freedom from any direct State or political mission," and the freedom to administer its "internal affairs." Metropolitan Antonii also favored granting the parish the status of "legal person" with the right to own property, while deeming it appropriate for the clergy to participate in *zemstvo* activities. One or more bishops were to hold seats in the State Council and have direct access to the Committee of Ministers.[4]

The memorandum's moderate tone and demands reflected more than a desire for greater independence; it expressed the hierarchy's dissatisfaction with the overprocurator of the Holy Synod, who controlled all access to the tsar and his government. By its nature, a truly independent Church should have the right to speak for itself.

S. Iu. Witte, the chairman of the Committee of Ministers, sponsored a second statement on church reform presented to a special Conference on Ecclesiastical Affairs under the Committee of Ministers. Encouraged by Witte's sympathy, liberal academy professors had drafted a statement which was much more radical than Antonii's note. Labeling the Church's dependency "unlawful" (*nezakonyi*) since it kept Orthodoxy "in a state of paralysis," the Witte-sponsored memorandum went on to argue that *sobornost'* required lay participation in an eventual council and even in the election of candidates for the clergy.[5]

Finally, a third document, a liberal manifesto signed by

[4]Metropolitan Antonii's *zapiska* was published in *Slovo*, 28 March 1905, and reprinted in I.V. Preobrazhenskii, ed., *Tserkovnaia reforma: sbornik statei dukhovnoi i svetskoi periodicheskoi pechati po voprosu o reforme* (St. Petersburg, 1905) pp. 133-36

[5]Text in *Slovo*, 28 March 1905.

thirty-two priests of the capital and representing the opinion
of leading married clergy, demanded the convocation of a
council with an unspecified agenda, which, however, could
include such items as the election of bishops by their dioceses.[6]

Emboldened by public opinion and led by Metropolitan
Antonii, the Holy Synod requested the tsar to authorize a
"local," that is, a national, council of bishops. According to
canons 4 and 5 of the Council of Nicaea, it was to be held
semi-annually, but in Russia none had met in two hundred
years. Acting upon Overprocurator K.P. Pobedonostsev's
advice, Nicholas II refused to grant the Synod's request.
Meanwhile, the old overprocurator attempted to delay the
reform movement by insisting that the bishops be consulted
about the issues. He expected no opposition from a presum-
ably docile and reactionary episcopate to any departure from
existing practice. Such is the origin of the *Replies.* The
responses actually reached St. Petersburg after the momentous revolutionary events of fall 1905, including the dismissal
of Pobedonostsev. In January 1906, a preconciliar commission,
whose existence implied the restoration of *sobornost'* in the
Russian Church, began to prepare for a national council.
Many of the most influential bishops expected it to meet after
Easter 1906.[7]

The bishops' *Replies* included a number of important
topics, especially the composition of the future council. Essentially the debate centered on the possible extension of voting
rights beyond the bishops to the clergy and laymen. The
bishops' ideas reflected the view frequently appearing in the
press.[8] They also discussed the merits of decentralized ecclesiastical administration, the reform of central administration
and the possible restoration of the patriarchate, and the extent
of competence of ecclesiastical courts (particularly in marital
affairs). Given the prominence of lower clergy and laymen
in discussions about reform, it is perhaps not surprising to
see the bishops deliberating the virtues of regular assemblies

[6]Text in *Tserkovnyi vestnik* (1905) p. 11; reproduced in *Tserkovnaia
reforma*, pp. 1-6.

[7]*Otzyvy eparkhial'nykh arkhiereev*, III, 276. This was the opinion of Sergii
(Stragorodskii), archbishop of Finland.

of clergy and laity and the degree to which the clergy should be encouraged to take a more active part in the life and responsibilities of society. The parish (as the nucleus of the Church) and its canonical and legal status also came under the bishops' close scrutiny. Several areas, such as church property (its acquisition and alienation), theological education, and liturgical practice and church discipline, held special interest for the bishops. A large majority voiced dissatisfaction with the inaccessibility of much of the liturgical rites in the mass of the faithful, with a minority suggesting that the texts be translated from Church Slavonic into modern Russian. Nearly every bishop demanded modifications for achieving the congregation's fuller participation in liturgical worship.[9]

The bishops did not deal directly with the problem of Church-state relations, but that issue appears clearly in the background, particularly in relation to proposed decentralization, the reform of church courts, and the participation of clergymen in society. Since a full analysis of the *Replies* would require more space than is available here, only a few brief remarks on these three areas can be offered. These, however, may suffice to encourage others to make fuller use of the abundant materials found in the *Replies*.

The creative and canonical discussions of reform naturally focused on institutions. Only three bishops believed that the existing system of church administration should continue unchanged. Apparently their conservative reaction reflected a fear of reform in the midst of revolutionary unrest. Bishop Lavrentii of Tula, one of the three conservatives, declared that "division of the church—as well as that of the state—can in no case be approved, especially in the present moment of trouble."[10]

[8]Cf. Paul Valliere's study on "The Idea of a Council in Russian Orthodoxy in 1905," *Russian Orthodoxy under the Old Regime*, eds. R.L. Nichols and G. Stavrou (Minneapolis, MN: University of Minnesota Press, 1978).

[9]This aspect of the *Replies* will not be discussed here; the liturgical and disciplinary reforms suggested by the bishops are particularly emphasized in the only (and very brief) existing survey of the *Replies* by N. Zernov, "The Reform of the Church and the Pre-revolutionary Russian Episcopate," *St. Vladimir's Seminary Quarterly* 6 (1962) 3:128-38 (originally published in N. Berdiaev's periodical *Put'*, Paris, 1934).

[10]*Otzyvy*, 3, 387.

The rest of the Russian episcopate unanimously favored the establishment of ecclesiastical provinces headed by regional metropolitans and with regional synods of bishops having autonomy. Undoubtedly the unpopularity of the centralized synodal bureaucracy headed by a lay overprocurator accounts for this remarkable consensus; yet the bishops also wished to restore a system more in conformity with canon law and church tradition. Certainly the historical studies of the early Church and its ministries published by the ecclesiastical academies gave the bishops (or the commissions appointed to draft the *Replies*) material which they utilized.[11] The responses generally asserted that ecclesiastical provinces would give the Church more independence, while reorganization would allow it to practice regular conciliarity (*sobornost'*), an objective less easily realized on the national level.[12]

Each ecclesiastical province was to have a canonically based synod, empowered to elect bishops and hear complaints against them. Such complaints, if serious enough, could lead to a bishop's deposition. The crucial issue implied in decentralization was the Church's dependence on the state: since Peter I, all bishops had been appointed by a decree of the Holy Synod, which was, in fact, an organ of the state. On this point, several bishops quoted apostolic canon 30,[13] which considers invalid any episcopal appointment "by worldly rulers"; interpreted literally, it would actually mean that *all* the episcopal appointments since Peter were invalid! Few, however, advocated that it be so applied.

Thus, while basing their proposals on ancient canonical tradition, the *Replies* had to avoid unrealistic and artificial attempts at copying the structure of the early Church, which existed under different historical conditions. Several influential bishops were aware of this fact and pointed to the twentieth-century requirement of the Russian Church: reestablishment

[11]The books most frequently quoted are A.P. Lebedev, *Dukhovenstvo drevnei vselenskoi tserkvi* (Moscow, 1905) and P. Gidulianov, *Mitropolity v pervye tri veka khristianstva* (Moscow, 1905), the second study being the much more substantial. The various ecclesiastical periodicals also devoted numerous articles to the issue during the period 1904-17.

[12]Cf. Nikanor of Perm, *Otzyvy*, 2, 389.

[13]For example, Konstantin of Samara, ibid., 1, 431.

of canonical *norms,* not slavish imitation of ancient structures.[14]
The old and respected Metropolitan Flavian of Kiev sum-
marized the problems and goals of the projected reform in
four points. (1) Dioceses closely tied to the central administration in St. Petersburg are actually isolated from each other
and are unable to meet regional pastoral problems. (2)
Conciliarity (*sobornost'*) must first be practiced in regions
and "neighborhoods," that is, in the ecclesiastical provinces
presided over by their metropolitans. (3) The existing centralized bureaucracy has assumed a power which canonically
belongs to the bishops of a region meeting in council. (4)
Reform would allow the creation of smaller and more numerous dioceses (in each *uezd*), thereby enabling bishops to be
effective pastors of their flocks, not inaccessible high admin-
istrators.[15] On this last point Archbishop Antonii of Volyn'
suggested that "auxiliary" bishops—an institution borrowed
recently from Western Christianity—be suppressed and more
numerous and smaller dioceses be established.[16]

A substantial number of *Replies* suggested that, in addition to the presiding metropolitan and bishops, the provincial
councils include clergy and laity although some wished to
grant them only a consultative role.[17] Antonii of Volyn' pro-
tested virulently against any "democratic" participation by
clergy and laity in councils, but his remarks are exceptional.[18]
Clearly, the pattern of debate about provincial councils con-
forms precisely to that surrounding the composition of a national council for the entire Russian Church—a debate then
going on in the theological periodicals.

The *Replies* also include specific plans for the future
ecclesiastical provinces, the number of which varies in the
proposals from seven to fifteen. Those who favored seven
provinces followed obvious geographic, ethnic, and historical

---

[14]Cf. the opinion of Professor A. Brilliantov, included in the remarks of
St. Petersburg Metropolitan Antonii, ibid., 3, 117; and Sergii of Finland, 3,
227.

[15]Ibid., 2, 103.

[16]Ibid., 1, 122.

[17]Stefan of Mogilev, ibid., 1 99-100; Simeon of Ekaterinoslav, 1 77; Flavian of Kiev, 2, 75.

[18]Ibid., 1, 112-20.

divisions.[19] Such provinces were to include the northwest (St. Petersburg), central Russia (Moscow), the South (Kiev), the Caucasus (Tiflis), Belorussia, the East (Kazan), and Siberia. Other bishops recommended further subdivisions of these vast areas.

The plans for ecclesiastical regionalism could not ignore the national diversity of the Russian Empire. In 1905 national awareness had not yet become a critical issue, but it appears in some of the *Replies*. As a Russian nationalist, Stefan of Mogilev mentioned the danger of Georgian separatism as a disadvantage of regionalism (which he otherwise supported) and suggested that the future "metropolitan of the Caucasus," exercising jurisdiction in areas distinct from those of the catholicos (national patriarch) of Georgia, always be a Russian.[20] The bishops of Belorussia and the Ukraine refer in passing to the need for preserving a unified "Russia." However, an opposite trend also found free expression. The exarch of Georgia openly claimed that traditional autocephaly (i.e., complete independence) should be restored to the Georgian Church. In his view, religious independence would not lead to political separatism.[21]

A further proposal for autonomy came from Tikhon, bishop of the Aleutian Islands and North America (and future patriarch of Moscow), who suggested that a separate (autocephalous) church in America be created. He argued that the Russian bishop of this diocese finds himself under completely different political conditions, for he is the head of a multinational religious body which includes not only Russian and Carpatho-Russian immigrants, but also Aleuts, Indians, Eskimos, as well as Serbs, Syrians, Greeks, and others.[22] Tikhon's project, which displayed a remarkable perception

[19]Cf. the *Replies* from Kursk, Perm, Volyn, Grodno, Olonets, Tomsk, Riazan, and America.

[20]Ibid., 1, 97.

[21]Ibid., 3, 510. Georgia, a country christianized in the fourth century, has been led by a "catholicos" since the sixth century. Political annexation by Russia early in the nineteenth century was followed by the suppression of this Georgian national patriarchate and the appointment of a Russian "exarch of Georgia."

[22]Ibid., 1, 531.

of the situation, subsequently served as an authoritative pattern for the creation of the American autocephalous church in 1970.

With the exception of only four bishops, the entire Russian episcopate in 1905 demanded restoration of the patriarchate suppressed by Peter the Great. Three of the dissenters apparently feared any substantial reform, including a council, in a revolutionary atmosphere.[23] The fourth, Paisii of Turkestan, belonged to the opposite extreme. He was afraid that a patriarch might be more easily controlled by the state than a collective body, and consequently he defended a collegiate and elective principle for all levels of church administration.[24]

While defending a restored patriarchate, the majority of bishops critized the "synodal" regime as uncanonical and contradicting the principle of *sobornost'*. A patriarch responsible for a conciliar form of government would assure the Church's independence from the centralized state bureaucracy.[25] Beyond these basic arguments, some *Replies* also reasoned that Orthodox tradition requires every national Church to be led personally by the bishop of its major city: among the Orthodox Churches, only the Russian Church since Peter I lacked this personal leadership.

However, the near unanimity in favor of the patriarchate did not extend to the description of the patriarch's role and responsibility. I. Sokolov, a learned historian of the patriarchate of Constantinople whose opinion on the canonical aspect of the projected reforms had been requested by the metropolitan of St. Petersburg, took the view that a patriarch acted as the head of a council.[26] The vast majority of the bishops, however, described the patriarch as only the "first among equals," so that the council of all the bishops would be the supreme authority, able to pass judgment upon the

[23]Parfenii of Podolsk, ibid., 2, 490; Lavrentii of Tula, 3, 381-82; Dimitrii, auxiliary of Podolsk, 2, 491.

[24]Ibid., 1, 50-52.

[25]See particularly the *Replies* from Ufa, 2, 54-55; Pskov, 2, 205-06; Kiev, 2, 103; Moscow, 3, 253-55; Warsaw, 2, 273; Riazan, 3, 577; Volyn', 3, 186-94; Orenburg, 2, 146-47; Kholm, 2, 466; and America, 1, 530.

[26]Ibid., 3, 128-29.

patriarch himself.[27] No unanimity emerged either among the bishops or in the Church as large on the issue of the future council's composition. Some favored a purely episcopal assembly; others insisted that it also include clergy and laity.

Clearly the *Replies* could not address or solve all problems of central church authority; they merely anticipated later discussions on the meaning of *sobornost'* and its possible institutional expressions which took place in the preconciliar meetings and in the ecclesiastical journals between 1905 and 1917. The solution finally accepted at the council of 1917-18 clearly determined that the patriarch was to be responsible to a council composed of bishops, clergy, and laity. However, the statute of 1917 also safeguarded the bishops' particular role by giving them a collective veto power over all the council's decisions. This solution (which resembles a sort of parliamentary bicameralism) was anticipated in the *Reply* by Archbishop Sergii of Finland (the future *locum tenens* and patriarch) when he suggested a procedure for patriarchal elections. Three candidates for patriarch were to be nominated respectively by the house of bishops, by the "lower" house of clergy and laity, and by the tsar. The patriarch would then be designated by lot.[28] It is worth noting that Patriarch Tikhon's election in October 1917 was accomplished by lot after nominations by the entire council (bishops, clergy, and laity, but not the tsar!).

Obviously in 1905 no bishops foresaw either the end of the monarchy or the separation of Church and state. Most of the *Replies* desired a benevolent, liberal Russian state in which the restored patriarchate would play an independent and socially meaningful role. The vast majority believed St. Petersburg would be the patriarch's normal residence. Only two bishops thought Moscow, the historic see of former Russian metropolitans and patriarchs, should again become the religious capital of Russia.[29]

An inevitable consequence of the system which reduced

[27]Cf., for example, the *Replies* from St. Petersburg, 3, 86; Moscow, 3, 256; Kaluga, 1, 29; Viatka, 2, 509; Kholm, 2, 466; Stavropol, 2, 261; Finland, 3, 260, 270; Orel, 1, 521; Orenburg, 2, 148; Irkutsk, 2, 227.

[28]Ibid., 3, 270.

[29]Ibid., Tambov, 3, 318; Finland, 3, 269.

the clergy to a closed caste (*soslovie*) was that the priest's role in Russian society became almost exclusively cultic. The formal administrative obligations to register births and marriages and a limited participation in the state educational system could not provide the clergy with a significant social function. Actually, there is some connection between contemporary Soviet legislation restricting the Church to "cultic" activities and the requirements of the Petrine system. The pre-Revolutionary Russian clergy's strong sense of being social outcasts certainly influenced, directly or indirectly, some of the demands and suggestions voiced in the *Replies*. Eventually this social question became the central issue and dominated the debates during the council of 1917-18. For this reason, too, most members of the council vigorously defended the recently developed system of prochial schools as a means for integrating Church and society more harmoniously, despite the fact that both the Duma and the Provisional Government considered these schools outdated and financially cumbersome. Another aspect of this same phenomenon can be seen in the "renovated" or "living" church of the 1920s, which to a large extent became a movement of "white clergy" and some socially oriented intellectuals against the most ascetic ideals represented by the monastically inclined episcopate. Only Antonii (Khrapovitskii) of Volyn' stood athwart this drive for greater social participation. His vituperative *Reply* in 1905 against "progressive," "republican," and "democratic" priests not only reflected his conservative ideology (in which he was not very consistent) but also his personal aristocratic background (quite exceptional among the bishops). He despised the clergy as a caste, but in this he stood very much alone.[30]

On the whole, the bishops in 1905 succeeded in avoiding such extreme positions and expressed only theological and pastoral considerations. A majority demanded that the clergy be given a voice in the political and social life of Russia, not as spokesmen for class interests but as witnesses of Christ's message. As citizens, it was thought members of the clergy should be given the right to participate in elections to the

[30]Ibid., 1, 112-20.

zemstvo, the city duma and the State Duma.[31] Election to such assemblies would assure that a responsible and articulate voice of the Church was heard.[32] These demands had already been presented in the memorandum of Antonii of St. Petersburg mentioned earlier. He had suggested that the patriarch and some bishops be *ex officio* members of the State Council.

While generally advocating a greater social role for the clergy, several bishops also warned against the dangers of politics, quoting ancient canons prohibiting the assumption of direct political power and legal financial responsibilities by priests. If elected to legislative bodies, they were to contribute to debates dealing with church building, education, welfare, and morality. Clergymen were not to participate in politics as such.[33] Interestingly enough, Bishop Evlogii of Kholm, subsequently a prominent and very active member of the State Duma, was among those who gave such warnings. Actually, the bishops were aware of the difficulty of precisely demarcating those "politics" forbidden to the clergy from those "social responsibilities" which are an unavoidable part of the Church's function. Clearly, but understandably, they lacked practical experience in such matters.

The content of the *Replies* by the Russian bishops in 1905 can be analyzed and criticized from different angles. From a theological standpoint, for example, the issue of the respective roles of bishops, lower clergy, and laity at a council, as it was discussed in the *Replies,* cannot be truly solved without first establishing basic ecclesiological presuppositions on the nature of local Churches (or dioceses), the manner of electing bishops, and the nature of the episcopal ministry. The notion of *sobornost'* is much too vague and insufficient to give an answer to concrete ecclesiological issues—the ecclesiological ideas underlying the *Replies* would thus require a separate study. Similarly, the influence exercised by the prevailing trends in social thought—toward liberal democracy, romantic "populism" (*norodnichestvo*), and conservatism— need serious analysis. Finally, the collection of the *Replies* is of

[31]Ibid., Chernigov, 1, 111.
[32]Ibid., Polotsk, 1, 137; Khar'kov, 1, 20; Kaluga, 1, 33; America, 1, 545.
[33]Ibid., Voronezh, 1, 45; Novgorod, 2, 20; Kholm, 2, 489; Kazan, 3, 436.

undeniable historical importance for the picture it gives of all the major personalities of Russian Church history in the revolutionary and post-relutionary era: Tikon (Bellavin) bishop of the Aleutian islands and North America, who became the first patriarch (1918-25); Sergii (Stragorodskii), archbishop of Finland, the future *locum tenens,* (1926-43) and patriarch (1943-44); Evlogii (Georgievskii), bishop of Kholm, later metropolitan of Western Europe (1922-46) and leader of the influential Russian Orthodox community in Paris; Antonii (Khrapovitskii), archbishop of Volyn, later metropolitan of Kiev, and eventually the head of the "Russian Orthodox Church in exile" in Sremski Karlovci, Yugoslavia; and many others. It should be noted that most of the *Replies* reflect the work of commissions established in dioceses, some of which, especially those working in such intellectual centers as St. Petersburg, Moscow, Kiev, and Kazan, where the local bishop could utilize the resources of the theological academies, have produced reports of great scholarly interest. Elsewhere, the work of the commissions reflects the trends among provincial clergy and church leadership.

All these elements contribute to making the collection of *Replies* probably the most representative and comprehensive document on the Russian Church's condition in the Old Regime's last years.

Index

Acholius, Bishop of Thessalonica, 126
Afanassieff, Nicholas, 134
Africa: East, 107; North, 114, 127
Akathistos Hymn to the Theotokos, 44
Alexandria, 104, 113, 123, 124, 126-33
Alexiad, 132
Alexis I, Emperor, 132
Allegorism, 35
Ambrose, Bishop of Milan, 121
Anastasius of Sinai, 24
Anamnesis, 17, 52, 55
Anselm, 68
Antioch, 123, 125, 126, 128-33
Antonii (Khrapovitskii), Archbishop of Volyn', 150, 154, 156
Antonii (Vadkovskii), Metropolitan of St. Petersburg, 146, 147, 155
Aphraates, 24
Apologists, 33, 43
Apostolic Succession, 28, 53, 55, 58-59, 60; in Ignatius and Irenaeus, 90, 91
Arabs, 77, 115
Areopagiticum, Corpus, 42
Arianism, 40, 112, 121, 122, 123
Arians, 57, 96
Arianzum, 126
Aristenos, 129
Aristotle, 44, 45
Athanasius, 16, 17, 71, 73, 122; accepted by Reformers, 77; quoted, 21
Augsburg Confession, 61, 69, 77
Augustine, 34-42, 66, 80; place in Christian tradition, 33, 69, 70, 72, 75, 76; thought of, 19, 45, 71, 73

Aulen, 68
Autocephaly, 109-110, 130, 131, 151, 152

Balsamon, 129, 130, 133
"Baptism, Eucharist and Ministry," 59, 62
Barth, Karl, 80
Basil of Caesarea, 16, 40, 43, 127; accepted by Reformers, 77; writings, 17, 57, 125
Bishops, succession of, 26
Bultmann, 80

Canaan, 104
Canons, 111-16
Calvin, John, 65, 69, 75; condemnation of, 79; thought of, 70, 73
Cappadocian Fathers, *see also* Basil of Caesarea, Gregory of Nazianzus, Gregory of Nyssa; 39, 123, 124; theology of 18, 41, 42
Catholicossate of Seleucia-Ktesiphon, 32
Celestine, Pope, 114
Christus Victor, 68
Comnena, Anna, 132-33
Conciliarity, *see also* Sobornost'; 142
"Confession of Dositheos", 79
Confessionalism, 61, 94
Confessions, 38
Congregationalism, 55
Constantine, Emperor, 112
Constantinople, 113, 121, 123-34, 136-38
Councils: ecumenical, 100; First Ecumenical (Nicaea, 325), 112, 121, 135; Second Ecumenical (Constantinople, 381), 113, 121, 124-27, 137, 138; Third Ecumen-

ical (Ephesus, 431), 34, 114, 115; Fourth Ecumenical (Chalcedon, 451), 136, 137, 138; Fifth Ecumenical (Constantinople, 553), 34, 39; Sixth Ecumenical (Quinisext, *in Trullo*, 692), 114, 115; Antioch (168), 122, 123; Aquileia (382), 126; Bethlehem (1675), 79; Carthage (419), 114; Constantinople (1872), 141; Florence, 99; Lyons, Second of, 98; Moscow (1917-18), 146; Rome (382), 127; Sardica (343), 136, 137; St. Sophia (879-80), 137; Trent, 99; forthcoming, 109-110

Creation, 35, 40, 41, 42, 85; Augustine's and Origen's views of, 35, 37

Creeds, 7, 8, 17, 18, 25

Crusades, 77

Cyprian of Carthage, 27, 55, 135

Cyprus, 114, 115

Cyril and Methodius, 8, 139

Cyril Loukaris, 79

Cyril of Alexandria, 42

Cyzicus, 115, 116

Damasus, Pope, 127

Deification, *see also* Theosis, 16, 21

Denominationalism, 61, 94

Department of Orthodox Confession, 143

Diaspora, 104-7, 110, 140

Dionysius the Areopagite, 33, 43

Disunity, 138, 139

Donatists, 56

Dyophysites, 74

Ecclesiology, 54, 136; eucharistic, 118, 134, 135; in ecumenism, 52, 56, 59, 81; Protestant, 75, 76

Eckhardt, 69

Ecumenical Debate, 29, 52

Ecumenical Movement, 11, 81, 93-94, 106

Ecumenical Patriarchate, 104

Ecumenism, 10, 61

Encratites, 57

Enlightenment, the, 87

Enneads, 36

Ephrem the Syrian, 24

Epiphanius, 77

Episcopacy, 63, 135-36; monarchical, 28, 54, 55, 134

Eschaton, 27, 101

Eucharist, 60, 62, 91, 117; divine presence in, 55, 96, 135; eschatological dimension of, 85, 86, 105, 140-41; essence of the Church, 52-53, 90, 134; relation of episcopate to, 27, 54, 118

Evagrius Ponticus, 35-36

Evlogii (Georgievskii), Bishop of Kholm, 155, 156

Exegesis, 34, 95, 98

Exhortation to Youth as to How They Shall Best Profit by the Writings of Pagan Authors, 43

Fall, the, 35, 40, 72, 73, 76

Femininity, 24

Filaret (Drozdov), Metropolitan of Moscow, 145

Filioque, 18, 78, 96, 99

Flavian, Metropolitan of Kiev, 150

Florovsky, Georges, 46, 78

Free Will, 68

Gnosticism, 26-27, 91

Gnostics, 57, 85, 89

Grace, 75, 92, 120; in Eastern theology, 39, 71, 73; in Western theology, 37, 67, 68, 69, 76

Gratian, Emperor, 121

Gregory, accepted by Reformers, 77

Gregory I, Pope, 136

Gregory VII, Pope, 132

Gregory of Nazianzus, 16, 22, 123-27

Gregory of Nyssa, 22, 39, 40, 41

Gregory Palamas, 19

Harnack, Adolf, 32

Hellenism, 31-47

History of the Ecumenical Patriarchate, 134

Hussites, 50

Iconoclasm, 44

Iconoclasts, 96

Ignatius of Antioch, 55, 63, 134; quoted, 7, 54, 117; role of, 90-93; thought of, 27, 53, 118

Incarnation, 21, 41, 116

"International Orthodox Missionary Society," 106

Irenaeus of Lyons, 41, 73; accepted by Reformers, 77; quoted, 21, 28; role of, 90-93; thought of, 26, 27, 56

Izois, 57

Jeremiah II, Patriarch of Constantinople, 50, 77-78

John VIII, Pope, 137

John Chrysostom, 69, 85

Julian of Eclana, 66

Justinian I, Emperor, 33, 42

Justinian II, Emperor, 115

Justinianopolis, 115

Kenosis, 25

Khomyakov, A. S., 8, 74, 145

Kingdom of God, 52, 62, 106, 114; in apocalyptism, 86-87; in Church, 27, 53

Küng, 97

Kydones, Demetrios, 45, 46

Lavrentii, Bishop of Tula, 148

Leo I, Pope, 136

Letters to Serapion, 16

Lord's Day, 53

Lord's Supper, *see also* Eucharist; 116

Love, 11, 19, 25, 117

Lucifer of Cagliari, 123, 125

Luther, Martin, 63, 65, 75; and Orthodoxy, 49, 50, 79; thought of, 60, 68, 70, 72

Lutherans, 50, 51, 60; merger of two denominations in, 61

Macarius the Great, 23; ps.-Macarius, 22

Macrina, 40

Magisterium, 28, 67, 69, 90

Manicheism, 38; dualism of, 36, 66

Maximos, Metropolitan of Sardis, 134

Maximus the Confessor, 22, 39

Maximus the Cynic, 124, 126, 127

Melanchton, Philip, 50, 77

Meletius, Bishop of Antioch, 123, 125, 126

Meno, 36

Millet, Christian, 138

Mission, 103-6, 108, 139, 142; in Origen and Augustine, 35, 37; not adopted by all, 32, 45, 140; place of in Church, 31, 46, 47

Missouri Synod, 62

Modalism, 122

Mongol Invasion, 77

Monophysites, 74, 96

Muslims, 103, 104

Nectarius, 126

Neoplatonism, 22, 33, 35-37, 40

Nestorians, 74, 96

New Valaamo Assembly (1979), 107, 109

Nicaeans: neo-, 122, 123; old- 122, 123

Nicholas II, Tsar, 147

Niebuhr, Reinhold, 95

Novatians, 57, 112-13

Occam, 69

Old Believers, 74, 138

Old-Calendarists, Greek, 74

On the Holy Spirit, 16

On the Incomprehensibility of God, 69

On the Soul and the Resurrection, 40

Origen, 33, 34-42, 122

Original Sin, 66, 78

Ottoman Empire, 138

Paganism, 44

Pagans, 103

Paisii, Bishop of Turkestan, 152

Papacy, 96-97

Paul VI, Pope, 98, 99

Paulinus, Bishop of Antioch, 123, 125-27

Pelagianism, 38

Pelagius, 66

Pelikan, Jaroslav, 40

Peter, Apostle, 55

Peter the Great, 143, 144, 145, 149, 152

Philotheos, Patriarch, 137

Photius, Patriarch of Constantinople, 18, 137

Phyletism, 141, 142

Plato, 36-37, 44

Platonism, 35, 38, 42, 45, 85

Plotinus, 36-37
Pluralism, 139
Plurality, 142
Pneumatomachoi, 125
Pobedonostsev, K. P., Overprocurator, 144, 146, 147
Post-Christian, 87, 92
Predestination, 37
Presidents of local churches, 54
Prestige, G. L., 16
Prophecy, 88

Reform, 144, 145
Reformation, 49, 65
Replies (*Otzyvy*), 144, 147-56
Resurrection, 40, 41, 62
Rome, 121, 127, 131-33, 136-38; New, 121; Third, 138

Sabellian Modalism, 40
Saints, 88; communion of, 88, 93
Salvation, 68
Saturninus, 57
Schisms, *see also* Arians, Donatists, Encratites, Gnostics, Iconoclasts, Monophysites, Nestorians, Old Believers, Old Calandarists; 10, 49, 56-57, 74, 77, 79, 81
Scholarios, Gennadios, 45, 46
Scholasticism, 34, 45, 67, 68, 69, 75
Semitic Christianity, 32
Seraphim of Sarov, 26
Sergii, (Stragorodoskii), Archbishop of Finland, 153, 156
Slavonic, Church, 148
Sobornost', 8, 145-47, 149-50, 152-53, 155
Socialism, 101
Sokolov, I., 152

Sophiologists, 80
Stefan, Bishop of Mogilev, 151
Symeon the New Theologian, 23
Syndesmos, 106-7, 109
Synergy, 75, 86
Synodikon of Orthodoxy, 44

Tauler, 69
Theodoret, 77
Theodosius I the Great, Emperor, 122, 124, 125
Theosis, *see also* Deification; 19, 39
Thomas Aquinas, 67
Thomism, 45, 67, 69, 80
Tikhon (Bellavin), Bishop of Aleutian Islands and North America, 151, 153, 156
Timaeus, 36
Timothy of Alexandria, 126
Trajan, Emperor, 53
Trinity, analogies of, 19, 38

Unity, 109-110

Vatican I, 99
Vatican II, 97, 99, 139

Westminster Confession, 61
World Council of Churches, 59, 82, 94
Wisconsin Synod, 62
Witte, S. Iu., 146

Yannoulatos, Anastasios, 107

Zion, 31
Zizioulas, John, 27, 134
Zonaras, John, 129, 132-33